TOKYO, KYOTO & OSAKA GUIDE

Most Recent Tokyo, Kyoto and Osaka 2024-2025 Travel Guide

JAMES K PALMER

3

TABLE OF CONTENT

Introduction

Welcome to the enchanting world of Japan, where modernity seamlessly blends with ancient traditions, and each city tells a unique tale of history and innovation. As you embark on your journey through Tokyo, Kyoto, and Osaka, this travel guide aims to be your companion, offering insights and tips that cater to both first-time visitors and seasoned travelers seeking new adventures.

Discovering Tokyo: A Metropolis of Contrasts

Tokyo, the pulsating heart of Japan, beckons with its towering skyscrapers, historic temples, and bustling streets. In this sprawling metropolis, you'll find a harmonious blend of futuristic technology and time-honored customs. Dive into the vibrant neighborhoods of Shibuya and Shinjuku, where the neon lights compete with the energy of the crowd. Explore the tranquility of Asakusa, home to the iconic Senso-ji Temple, a testament to Tokyo's rich cultural heritage. Our guide will lead you through the city's diverse districts, each offering a distinct flavor of Tokyo's multifaceted identity.

Tokyo

Journey Through Kyoto

Kyoto, a city steeped in history and tradition, welcomes you with its serene gardens, majestic temples, and timeless tea ceremonies. As you wander through the historic Gion district, you'll encounter geishas gracefully making their way through narrow cobblestone streets. Immerse yourself in the contemplative beauty of Kinkaku-ji (the Golden Pavilion) and the serene Arashiyama Bamboo Grove. Kyoto's essence lies in its ability to transport you to a bygone era while coexisting with the contemporary world. Our guide unveils the hidden gems and cultural wonders that make Kyoto a captivating destination.

Osaka: A Culinary and Entertainment Extravaganza

Osaka, known as the "Nation's Kitchen," is a gastronomic paradise where street food reigns supreme. From the bustling stalls of Dotonbori to the historic Osaka Castle, the city offers a dynamic blend of flavors and entertainment. Discover the unique "kuidaore" spirit, encouraging visitors to eat until they drop. Osaka's vibrant nightlife, amusement parks, and modern attractions ensure there's never a dull moment. Our guide navigates you through the city's culinary delights, cultural hotspots, and lively atmosphere, ensuring your time in Osaka is filled with unforgettable experiences.

Kyoto

Navigating the Seasons:
Japan's distinct seasons add a layer of wonder to your journey. Experience the ephemeral beauty of cherry blossoms in spring, savor the vibrant hues of autumn leaves, and witness the enchanting winter illuminations. Our guide provides insights into the best times to visit each city, ensuring you capture the essence of Japan in its various seasonal splendors.

In the pages that follow, delve into the practicalities of planning your trip, uncover hidden gems, and immerse yourself in the cultural intricacies that make Tokyo, Kyoto, and Osaka truly extraordinary. Your adventure begins now, as you turn the pages and open the door to the captivating world of Japan. Enjoy the journey!

Welcome to Japan

Welcome to the Land of the Rising Sun! Japan awaits with open arms, ready to enchant you with its rich tapestry of tradition, innovation, and natural beauty. From the vibrant metropolis of Tokyo to the serene temples of Kyoto and the lively streets of Osaka, your journey is about to unfold in a country where ancient customs coexist harmoniously with cutting-edge technology.

Osaka

As you step onto Japanese soil, be prepared to immerse yourself in a culture that values courtesy, respect, and a deep appreciation for the arts. Whether you're a first-time visitor or a returning traveler, Japan's unique blend of old and new promises a captivating experience.

Throughout your stay, you'll encounter a culinary landscape that tantalizes the taste buds, from sushi and ramen to the delicate flavors of matcha. The landscapes, too, will leave you breathless — from the cherry blossom-strewn parks in spring to the snow-covered landscapes in winter.

This guide is your key to unlocking the wonders of Tokyo, Kyoto, and Osaka. It's designed to be your companion, offering practical tips, cultural insights, and recommendations to ensure your journey is not just a trip but a memorable adventure.

So, as you embark on this exploration of Japan, let the sakura blossoms guide your way, and may the vibrant spirit of the country leave an indelible mark on your heart. Welcome to Japan – where tradition meets modernity, and each moment is an opportunity for discovery and delight. Enjoy your stay!

Overview of Tokyo, Kyoto, and Osaka

Tokyo:

Tokyo, Japan's bustling capital, is a mesmerizing blend of innovation and tradition. Skyscrapers punctuate the skyline, housing cutting-edge technology and contemporary fashion, while historic temples and shrines provide glimpses into the city's cultural past. From the neon lights of Shibuya Crossing to the serenity of Ueno Park, Tokyo offers a diverse tapestry of experiences. Explore world-class dining, vibrant entertainment, and a seamless fusion of the ultramodern and the timeless.

Kyoto:

Nestled amidst scenic landscapes, Kyoto is a living testament to Japan's rich cultural legacy. This city, once the imperial capital, exudes an air of tranquility and refinement. Discover ancient temples, traditional tea ceremonies, and the iconic geisha culture in the historic Gion district. Kyoto's atmospheric charm, coupled with its picturesque gardens and historic architecture, transports visitors to a bygone era, making it a captivating destination for those seeking cultural immersion.

Osaka:
Known as the "Kitchen of Japan," Osaka boasts a reputation for its delectable street food and culinary delights. The city's vibrant street life and modern entertainment complexes, such as Universal Studios Japan, create an energetic atmosphere. Osaka Castle stands as a symbol of the city's rich history, while the bustling Dotonbori district showcases the vivacious spirit of urban Japan. Experience the warmth of Osaka's locals, known for their friendliness, as you indulge in gastronomic adventures and explore the city's dynamic charm.

Each city, Tokyo, Kyoto, and Osaka, offers a distinctive flavor of Japan. From the futuristic allure of Tokyo to the historical elegance of Kyoto and the lively urban energy of Osaka, your journey through these cities promises a diverse and unforgettable experience. Embrace the contrasts, savor the unique offerings, and let the essence of each city leave an indelible mark on your travel memories.

Traveling Seasons and Weather Guide

Japan's diverse climate adds a captivating layer to your travel experience, with each season offering unique charms. Whether you're captivated by cherry blossoms, enchanted by fall foliage, or drawn to winter illuminations, here's a guide to help you navigate Japan's weather throughout the year.

1. Spring (March to May): Cherry Blossom Spectacle
Spring heralds the iconic cherry blossom season, or "sakura." Parks and gardens burst into hues of pink and white, creating a magical atmosphere. Mild temperatures make it an ideal time for exploration. Pack layers and join locals for hanami (flower viewing) picnics under blooming cherry trees.

2. Summer (June to August): Warm and Humid
Summer brings warm temperatures and high humidity. While it's festival season with lively celebrations like Gion Matsuri in Kyoto, be prepared for occasional rain. Light clothing and sunscreen are essential. Explore coastal areas or mountain retreats to escape the heat.

3. Autumn (September to November): Fall Foliage Extravaganza
Autumn paints Japan in vivid hues of red, orange, and gold as foliage peaks. The weather remains pleasant, and outdoor activities thrive. Explore temples and parks to witness the stunning momijigari (fall foliage viewing). A light jacket is advisable as temperatures gradually cool.

4. Winter (December to February): Crisp and Snowy
Winter unveils a different charm, especially in regions like Hokkaido. While Tokyo and Kyoto experience cooler temperatures, it's the perfect time for winter sports up north. Enjoy onsens (hot springs), winter festivals, and the enchanting beauty of snow-covered landscapes. Bundle up with layers, including a warm coat.

Practical Tips:

Check the specific weather forecast for each city on your itinerary.
Dress in layers to adapt to temperature variations throughout the day.
Carry an umbrella and waterproof gear, especially during the rainy season.
Be mindful of peak travel times, such as Golden Week in late April to early May, and plan accommodations accordingly.

By understanding Japan's seasonal nuances, you can tailor your itinerary to align with your preferences, whether it's blooming flowers, vibrant festivals, or serene winter landscapes. Embrace the ever-changing beauty of Japan, where each season unfolds a new chapter in the country's natural splendor.

Chapter 1: Essential Planning

Embarking on a trip to Japan requires thoughtful preparation to ensure a seamless and enriching experience. From visa requirements to cultural nuances, here's a guide to essential planning for your exploration of Tokyo, Kyoto, and Osaka.

1. Visa and Entry Requirements:
   Check visa requirements based on your nationality.
   Ensure your passport is valid for the duration of your stay.
   Keep a copy of your travel itinerary and accommodation reservations.

2. Currency and Money Matters:
   Familiarize yourself with Japan's currency (Japanese Yen).
   Inform your bank about your travel dates to avoid card issues.
   Consider carrying some cash, as not all places accept cards.

3. Language and Cultural Tips:
   Learn basic Japanese phrases for communication.
   Familiarize yourself with Japanese customs and etiquette.

Bowing is a common greeting; a slight bow is polite in most situations.

4. Transportation Options:

Research transportation passes for cost-effective travel.

Learn how to navigate public transportation systems in each city.

Consider renting a pocket Wi-Fi or purchasing a local SIM card for internet access.

5. Airport Guide:

Plan your arrival and departure from major airports like Narita or Kansai.

Arrange transportation from the airport to your accommodation.

Explore duty-free shopping options for souvenirs.

6. Accommodation:

Book accommodations well in advance, especially during peak seasons.

Explore a variety of options, from traditional ryokans to modern hotels.

Check reviews and amenities to find the best fit for your preferences.

7. Must-Visit Attractions:

Create a list of key attractions in each city.

Prioritize based on your interests and time constraints.

Check for any special events or festivals during your visit.

8. Safety and Emergency Information:
Save emergency numbers and addresses in your phone.
Familiarize yourself with the location of embassies or consulates.
Carry a copy of your travel insurance details.

9. Health and Wellness:
Ensure you have necessary vaccinations.
Carry any required medications and a basic first aid kit.
Stay hydrated and be mindful of any dietary restrictions.

10. Packing Essentials:
Pack according to the season and expected weather.
Comfortable walking shoes are crucial for exploring.
Consider a universal power adapter for your electronic devices.

As you meticulously plan each aspect of your journey, remember to leave room for spontaneity and the joy of discovery. Japan's rich tapestry awaits, and with thorough planning, you're poised for an adventure filled with cultural immersion and unforgettable moments. Safe travels!

Visa and Entry Requirements

Before embarking on your journey to Japan, it's essential to understand the visa and entry requirements to ensure a smooth entry into the country. Here's a comprehensive guide to help you navigate this crucial aspect of your travel planning:

1. Visa Requirements:
   Tourist Visa: Most visitors to Japan can enter visa-free for short stays (up to 90 days) for tourism, business, or family visits. However, specific countries may require a visa.
   Visa-Exempt Countries: Check if your country is on the list of visa-exempt countries or if it qualifies for a visa waiver program.

2. Visa Application Process:
   If a visa is required, initiate the application process well in advance.
   Contact the nearest Japanese embassy or consulate to obtain the necessary application forms and information.
   Provide accurate and complete information, including details about your itinerary, accommodation, and purpose of visit.

3. Required Documents:
   Common documents include a valid passport, completed visa application form, passport-size photos, flight itinerary, accommodation reservations, and proof of financial means.

Check for specific requirements based on your nationality.

4. Visa Fees:

Verify the visa processing fee and payment methods accepted by the embassy or consulate.

Be prepared to pay the fee when submitting your application.

5. Visa Processing Time:

Start the visa application process well in advance, as processing times vary.

Consider peak travel seasons, such as cherry blossom season, which may lead to longer processing times.

6. Visa Extension:

If you plan to stay longer than initially allowed, inquire about the possibility of extending your visa.

Extension procedures vary, and it's essential to follow the guidelines provided by Japanese immigration authorities.

7. Arrival Procedures:

Upon arrival in Japan, go through immigration and present your passport and any required documents.

Follow the entry procedures as instructed by immigration officers.

8. Electronic Travel Authorization (ETA):

Some countries may have electronic travel authorization systems in place, allowing for a simplified entry process.

Check if your nationality qualifies for an ETA and follow the application process.

Ensure you stay informed about the latest updates on visa requirements and entry regulations. Taking the time to understand and fulfill these requirements will contribute to a hassle-free and enjoyable experience as you explore the wonders of Japan. Safe travels!

Currency and Money Matters

Navigating the currency and financial landscape in Japan is an essential aspect of your travel preparation. Here's a comprehensive guide to help you manage your finances effectively during your exploration of Tokyo, Kyoto, and Osaka:

1. Japanese Yen (JPY):
   The official currency of Japan is the Japanese Yen.
   Familiarize yourself with the currency denominations, including coins (yen) and bills (sen).

2. Cash is King:
   While credit cards are widely accepted in urban areas, carrying cash is recommended, especially in more rural or traditional locations.
   ATMs are prevalent in cities, and international credit/debit cards can be used for withdrawals.

3. Notify Your Bank:
   Inform your bank about your travel dates and destinations to avoid card issues.

Check for any foreign transaction fees associated with your cards.

4. Currency Exchange:
Exchange currency at airports, banks, or authorized currency exchange offices.
Rates may vary, so compare options to get the best value.

5. Budgeting and Expenses:
Plan your budget in advance, considering accommodation, transportation, meals, and activities.
Keep a mix of small and large denominations for convenience.

6. Prepaid Travel Cards:
Consider using prepaid travel cards for added convenience and security.
These cards can be loaded with a specific amount and used like a debit card.

7. Tipping Culture:
Tipping is not a common practice in Japan and may even be considered rude.
Exceptional service is already included in the overall cost.

8. Tax-Free Shopping:
Look for stores displaying "Tax-Free" signs, especially when making significant purchases.

Foreign tourists are eligible for tax exemptions on certain goods.

9. Mobile Payments:
Mobile payment options like Suica or Pasmo cards are convenient for public transportation and small purchases.
Ensure your smartphone is set up for contactless payments if you plan to use these services.

10. Emergency Cash:
Have a backup plan for emergency cash, such as traveler's checks or a hidden stash.
Some rural areas may have limited ATM accessibility.

By understanding the currency dynamics and adopting a flexible approach to payments, you'll be well-equipped to handle money matters during your Japanese adventure. Whether strolling through vibrant markets or exploring high-tech districts, having a mix of cash and electronic payment options ensures a seamless and enjoyable travel experience.

Language and Cultural Tips

As you embark on your journey through Tokyo, Kyoto, and Osaka, immersing yourself in Japanese language and culture will enhance your travel experience. Here are essential language and cultural tips to help you navigate and connect with the local customs:

1. Learn Basic Japanese Phrases:
   Greetings: Master common phrases like "Konnichiwa" (Hello), "Arigatou gozaimasu" (Thank you), and "Sumimasen" (Excuse me).
   Politeness: Use "san" after a person's name for politeness, e.g., "Tanaka-san."
   Simple Requests: Familiarize yourself with phrases for ordering food, asking for directions, and seeking assistance.

2. Bowing Etiquette:
   Bowing is a common form of greeting and expressing gratitude.
   A slight bow is appropriate in most situations, while deeper bows are reserved for formal occasions.

3. Shoe Etiquette:
   Remove your shoes when entering someone's home, traditional accommodations (ryokans), or certain establishments.
   Use the provided slippers inside homes or specific areas.

4. Queuing Culture:
Japanese people value orderly queues.
Wait your turn in lines for public transportation, attractions, and services.

5. Public Transportation Manners:
Keep conversations low and set your phone to silent mode.
Give up your seat for elderly or disabled passengers.

6. Cash Transactions:
Hand cash or cards with both hands when making transactions.
Receive items with both hands as a sign of respect.

7. Onsen Etiquette:
Before entering an onsen (hot spring), thoroughly wash and rinse your body at the shower stations.
Tattoos may be frowned upon, so check onsen policies.

8. Photography Courtesy:
Ask for permission before taking photos of people, especially in rural areas.
Avoid photographing certain locations, such as inside temples.

9. Respect for Nature:
Dispose of trash responsibly, as public trash bins are scarce.
Show respect in natural settings, especially during cherry blossom and fall foliage seasons.

10. Silence in Public Spaces:
   Keep conversations hushed in public spaces, including public transportation.
   Use headphones when listening to music or watching videos.

11. Dress Modestly:
   Dress modestly when visiting temples and shrines.
   Avoid revealing clothing, especially in traditional settings.

12. Gift-Giving Etiquette:
   Present and receive gifts with both hands as a sign of respect.
   Open gifts privately to avoid appearing overly eager.

By embracing these language and cultural tips, you'll not only navigate Japan with ease but also forge meaningful connections with the locals. Respect for traditions and customs enhances the richness of your travel experience, ensuring you leave with cherished memories of Japan's warm hospitality and cultural diversity.

Chapter 2: Getting There

Embarking on your journey to Tokyo, Kyoto, and Osaka involves careful planning and consideration of transportation options. Whether you're arriving from an international destination or navigating within Japan, here's a comprehensive guide to help you get there seamlessly.

1. International Flights:
   Major Airports: Tokyo's Narita International Airport and Osaka's Kansai International Airport are key entry points for international travelers. Kyoto is conveniently accessed via Osaka.
   Airlines: Numerous international carriers operate flights to and from Japan, providing a range of options for direct and connecting flights.

2. Domestic Flights:
   Connecting Cities: Domestic flights are available between major cities, offering a quicker alternative to Shinkansen (bullet trains) for longer distances.
   Regional Airports: Consider using domestic flights to reach closer regional airports for specific destinations.

3. Shinkansen (Bullet Train):
   Efficient Rail Network: Japan's Shinkansen network is renowned for its speed and efficiency. The Tokaido Shinkansen connects Tokyo to Kyoto and Osaka in approximately 2 to 3 hours.

Rail Pass Options: JR Passes offer cost-effective options for unlimited travel on JR lines, including most Shinkansen routes.

4. Public Transportation within Cities:
Tokyo: The extensive Tokyo Metro and Toei Subway networks cover the city comprehensively. Buses and taxis are also readily available.

Kyoto: Public buses, Kyoto City Subway, and taxis provide convenient transportation within the city.

Osaka: The Osaka Metro, buses, and taxis offer efficient options for exploring the city.

5. Long-Distance Buses:
Affordable Travel: Long-distance buses are a budget-friendly alternative, connecting major cities and rural areas.

Highway Buses: Comfortable overnight highway buses offer a cost-effective way to travel between cities.

6. Rental Cars:
Exploring at Your Pace: Renting a car provides flexibility, especially for exploring rural areas or regions with limited public transportation.

International Driving Permit: Ensure you have the necessary documents, including an International Driving Permit.

7. Ferries and Boats:
Island Hopping: Ferries connect islands like Miyajima and Okinawa to the mainland.

Scenic Cruises: Enjoy scenic boat rides, such as the Sumida River Cruise in Tokyo.

8. Walking and Cycling:

Urban Exploration: Many attractions in Tokyo, Kyoto, and Osaka are within walking distance of each other.

Bike Rentals: Kyoto, in particular, offers bike rentals for a leisurely exploration of its historic streets.

9. Navigating Airports:

Transportation Hubs: Narita and Kansai airports have efficient transportation options, including trains and buses, connecting to city centers.

Navigating Haneda Airport: Tokyo's Haneda Airport is conveniently located, providing various transportation choices.

Planning your journey involves considering the most suitable transportation modes based on your preferences, budget, and schedule. Whether you opt for the efficiency of bullet trains, the convenience of domestic flights, or the scenic routes by ferry, each mode offers a unique perspective on the diverse landscapes of Japan. As you navigate the path to Tokyo, Kyoto, and Osaka, the transportation options seamlessly weave into the tapestry of your travel adventure. Enjoy the journey!

Transportation Options in Kyoto

Kyoto, with its historic temples, traditional tea houses, and picturesque landscapes, invites exploration by various transportation modes. Here's a guide to navigating the cultural heart of Japan through Kyoto's diverse transportation options:

1. Kyoto City Bus:
    Extensive Network: Kyoto's extensive bus network covers the city comprehensively, making it convenient for reaching various attractions.
    Bus Passes: Consider purchasing a Kyoto City Bus One-Day Pass for unlimited rides within a specified timeframe.

2. Kyoto City Subway:
    Two Lines: The Kyoto Municipal Subway has two lines, the Karasuma Line and the Tozai Line, providing efficient transport to key areas.
    ICOCA Card: Use an ICOCA card for seamless travel on both buses and the subway.

3. Bicycle Rentals:
    Explore at Your Pace: Kyoto's flat terrain and numerous bike lanes make cycling a popular and enjoyable option.

Rental Shops: Numerous rental shops offer bicycles, allowing you to explore historic districts like Gion and Higashiyama.

4. Kyoto Bus Passes:
Kyoto Sightseeing Card: This pass allows unlimited use of buses and subways for one or two days, making it cost-effective for tourists.

Randen Tram: The pass often includes the Randen tram, connecting to Arashiyama and the Golden Pavilion.

5. Taxis:
Convenient for Short Trips: Taxis are readily available and convenient for reaching specific destinations quickly.

Notable Landmarks: Taxis are recommended for reaching locations not well-served by public transportation.

6. Walking:
Historic Districts: Kyoto's charm lies in its walkable historic districts. Explore Gion, Higashiyama, and Fushimi Inari Taisha on foot to fully appreciate the ambiance.

Guided Walking Tours: Join guided walking tours for insightful cultural experiences.

7. Rickshaws:

Traditional Experience: For a unique cultural experience, consider a rickshaw ride through iconic areas like Arashiyama or along the Philosopher's Path.

Guided Tours: Rickshaw pullers often provide information about the history and significance of the sites during the ride.

8. Trains to Outlying Areas:

JR Lines: Use Japan Rail Pass to access JR lines, connecting Kyoto to nearby cities and attractions.

Saga Scenic Railway: Experience the romantic Sagano Scenic Railway, offering picturesque views of Kyoto's outskirts.

9. Shared Shuttle Services:

Airport Transfers: Shared shuttle services provide convenient transportation between Kyoto and Kansai International Airport or Osaka International Airport.

Hotel Pick-Ups: Many services offer door-to-door transportation, saving you the hassle of navigating public transportation.

Kyoto's transportation options offer a seamless blend of modern efficiency and traditional charm. Whether you opt for the iconic Kyoto City Bus, explore historic districts by bike, or take a leisurely rickshaw ride, each mode contributes to the unique and enchanting experience of exploring this cultural gem in the heart of Japan.

Transportation Options in in Tokyo

Tokyo, a sprawling metropolis of modernity and tradition, provides an extensive array of transportation options to explore its vibrant neighborhoods, historic sites, and contemporary attractions. Here's a guide to navigating Tokyo's diverse transportation network:

1. Tokyo Metro:
   Extensive Subway Network: The Tokyo Metro is a well-connected subway system, covering key areas in the city.
   IC Cards: Utilize IC cards like Suica or Pasmo for convenient access to both the metro and buses.

2. Japan Railways (JR):
   JR Yamanote Line: This loop line connects major districts such as Shibuya, Shinjuku, and Ueno. The JR Pass is beneficial for unlimited travel on JR lines.
   Chuo-Sobu Line: Explore neighborhoods like Akihabara and Asakusa along the Chuo-Sobu Line.

3. Toei Subway:
   Additional Subway Options: Toei Subway operates several lines complementing the Tokyo Metro, expanding your reach to various neighborhoods.

Toei Bus: Toei also operates a network of buses covering specific routes.

4. Buses:
City Buses: Tokyo's city buses are an economical option, reaching areas not covered by the subway.
Express Buses: Long-distance and express buses connect Tokyo to other cities and prefectures.

5. Tokyo Monorail:
Access to Haneda Airport: The Tokyo Monorail offers a direct connection from Hamamatsucho Station to Haneda Airport.
Scenic Views: Enjoy panoramic views during the journey, especially when approaching Odaiba.

6. Taxis:
Convenient for Short Distances: Taxis are readily available and convenient for short distances, late-night travel, or reaching destinations not well-served by public transportation.
Taxi Apps: Consider using taxi-hailing apps for a more efficient experience.

7. Yurikamome Line:
Odaiba Access: The Yurikamome Line is an automated, elevated train providing access to Odaiba, offering scenic views of Tokyo Bay.
Connecting Attractions: Explore attractions like Palette Town and Tokyo Big Sight along this line.

8. Rental Bikes:
   Bicycle-Friendly City: Tokyo's flat terrain and bike-friendly roads make cycling a pleasant option.
   Rental Services: Various bike rental services are available, providing a unique way to explore neighborhoods like Asakusa and Ueno.

9. Water Buses:
   Sumida River Cruises: Water buses operate along the Sumida River, offering scenic views of Tokyo's landmarks like Tokyo Skytree and Asakusa.
   Odaiba Access: Some water buses connect Odaiba to other waterfront locations.

10. Limousine Buses:
   Airport Transfers: Limousine buses provide convenient transportation between Tokyo and Narita or Haneda airports.
   Hotel Drop-Offs: Many services offer direct hotel drop-offs for added convenience.

Navigating Tokyo's transportation options offers a dynamic and efficient experience, allowing you to explore the city's diverse neighborhoods, historic landmarks, and contemporary attractions with ease. Whether you're underground on the Tokyo Metro, enjoying the views from the Yurikamome Line, or navigating the streets by bike, each mode contributes to the vibrant tapestry of Tokyo's transportation network.

Transportation Options in in Osaka

Osaka, renowned as the "Nation's Kitchen" for its delectable street food and vibrant culinary scene, boasts a transportation network that efficiently connects its diverse districts. Here's a guide to navigating Osaka's transportation options:

1. Osaka Metro:
   Comprehensive Subway System: The Osaka Metro consists of multiple lines covering the city and providing efficient transportation.
   ICOCA Card: Use an ICOCA card for seamless travel on both the metro and buses.

2. Japan Railways (JR):
   Osaka Loop Line: The JR Osaka Loop Line connects major districts, including Osaka Castle and Umeda. The JR Pass is beneficial for unlimited travel on JR lines.
   Osaka Station: JR lines from Osaka Station connect to neighboring cities, making it a central transportation hub.

3. Hankyu and Hanshin Railways:
   Private Rail Networks: Hankyu and Hanshin Railways operate private lines connecting Osaka to surrounding areas like Kyoto and Kobe.

Umeda and Namba Stations: Both stations are major transportation hubs served by these private railway networks.

4. Osaka City Buses:

Extensive Bus Network: Osaka's city buses cover a wide range of routes, providing access to various neighborhoods and attractions.

Bus Passes: Consider purchasing an Osaka Enjoy Eco Card for unlimited bus rides within a specified time frame.

5. Taxis:

Convenient for Short Distances: Taxis are readily available and convenient for short distances or reaching specific destinations efficiently.

Taxi Stands: Utilize designated taxi stands or hail a taxi on the street.

6. Nankai Electric Railway:

Airport Access: The Nankai Electric Railway provides direct access from Kansai International Airport to Namba Station.

Namba Access: Explore Namba's entertainment district and popular attractions using this railway.

7. Osaka Monorail:

Access to Osaka Expo Park: The Osaka Monorail connects to Osaka Expo Park, offering access to various exhibitions and events.

Trade Fair Access: Convenient for those attending events at Intex Osaka, a major convention center.

8. Water Bus:
Scenic River Cruises: Water buses operate along the Okawa River, providing a scenic and leisurely way to explore Osaka's waterfront.
Osaka Castle Access: Some water buses connect Osaka Castle to other locations.

9. Rental Bikes:
Cycling in Osaka: Osaka's flat topography and bike-friendly infrastructure make cycling an enjoyable option.
Bike Rental Shops: Various rental shops offer bicycles for exploring districts like Dotonbori and Shin-Osaka.

10. Limousine Buses:
Airport Transfers: Limousine buses provide convenient transportation between Osaka and Kansai International Airport or Itami Airport.
Hotel Drop-Offs: Some services offer direct hotel drop-offs, saving you time and effort.

Navigating Osaka's transportation options allows you to delve into its culinary delights, vibrant neighborhoods, and cultural attractions. Whether you're exploring the city by metro, enjoying the views from water buses, or savoring the culinary scene on foot, each mode contributes to the dynamic and flavorful experience of Osaka, the culinary capital of Japan.

Tokyo Airport Guide

Tokyo, as a major international hub, is served by multiple airports catering to various destinations. Whether you're arriving or departing, understanding the airports' layouts, services, and transportation options is essential for a smooth travel experience. Here's your guide to navigating Tokyo's key airports:

1. Narita International Airport (NRT):
   Location: Located in Chiba, approximately 60 kilometers east of central Tokyo.
   Terminals: Narita has three terminals – Terminal 1, Terminal 2, and Terminal 3 (mainly for low-cost carriers).
   Services: Offers a wide range of services, including duty-free shopping, lounges, currency exchange, and baggage services.

2. Haneda Airport (HND):
   Location: Situated closer to central Tokyo, about 14 kilometers south of the city center.
   Terminals: Haneda has three terminals – Terminal 1, Terminal 2, and the International Terminal.
   International Flights: The International Terminal serves as the hub for international flights, offering convenient access to Tokyo.

Domestic Flights: Terminals 1 and 2 primarily handle domestic flights.

3. Transportation Options from Airports:
  Narita Airport:
    Narita Express (N'EX): Direct train service to major Tokyo stations like Tokyo, Shibuya, and Shinjuku.
    Airport Limousine Bus: Connects Narita to various Tokyo hotels and neighborhoods.
      Taxis: Available for convenient point-to-point transfers.
  Haneda Airport:
      Tokyo Monorail: Connects Haneda to Hamamatsucho Station, providing access to the Yamanote Line.
      Keikyu Line: Direct train services to Tokyo and Shinagawa stations.
      Airport Limousine Bus: Extensive network connecting Haneda to Tokyo's major districts.
    Taxis: Convenient for quick transfers to various parts of Tokyo.

4. Domestic Transfers:
  Connecting Flights: If you have a domestic connection, both airports offer efficient transit services.
    Shuttle Buses: Shuttle services are available for transferring between terminals at Narita and Haneda.

5. Airport Facilities:

Lounges: Multiple lounges in both Narita and Haneda for various airlines, offering comfortable amenities for travelers.

Duty-Free Shopping: Explore a diverse range of shops offering Japanese products, electronics, fashion, and more.

Restaurants: Enjoy a variety of culinary options, from traditional Japanese cuisine to international flavors.

Wi-Fi Access: Free Wi-Fi is available throughout the airports.

6. Practical Tips:

Currency Exchange: Currency exchange services are available at both airports.

Baggage Storage: Facilities for storing luggage are accessible for travelers with extended layovers.

Information Desks: Seek assistance from information desks for any queries or travel-related information.

Whether you're jetting off to explore Tokyo or bidding farewell to the city, navigating Narita or Haneda Airport efficiently is crucial. With a well-planned approach and knowledge of available services, your experience at these airports will be a seamless part of your Tokyo adventure. Safe travels!

Kyoto Airport Guide

Kyoto, as a city without its own airport, relies on neighboring airports for air travel connections. The primary gateway is Osaka's Kansai International Airport (KIX) or Osaka Itami Airport (ITM). Here's your guide to navigating these airports when traveling to Kyoto:

1. Kansai International Airport (KIX):
Location: Located on an artificial island in Osaka Bay, approximately 75 minutes by train from Kyoto.
Access to Kyoto: Take the JR Haruka Limited Express from KIX to Kyoto Station for direct access.
    Terminals: Kansai Airport has two terminals – Terminal 1 (mainly international flights) and Terminal 2 (domestic flights).
Services: Offers a range of services, including duty-free shopping, lounges, and multilingual assistance.

2. Osaka Itami Airport (ITM):
Location: Situated in Itami, approximately 50 minutes by train from Kyoto.
Access to Kyoto: Take the Osaka Monorail and transfer to a JR train at Hotarugaike Station or use the Hankyu Railway from Itami Station.
    Terminal: Osaka Itami primarily handles domestic flights.
Services: Provides services such as lounges, shopping, and dining options.

3. Transportation Options from Airports:

From Kansai International Airport (KIX):

JR Haruka Limited Express: Direct train service to Kyoto Station.

Nankai Railway: Another train option connecting KIX to Namba Station in Osaka, where you can transfer to a JR train for Kyoto.

Limousine Buses: Direct bus services to Kyoto, convenient for those with heavy luggage.

From Osaka Itami Airport (ITM):

Osaka Monorail and JR Lines: Utilize the Osaka Monorail to reach Hotarugaike Station, where you can transfer to a JR train for Kyoto.

Hankyu Railway: Take the Hankyu Railway from Itami Station for a connection to Kyoto.

4. Domestic Transfers:

Connecting Flights: If arriving at Osaka Itami Airport and connecting domestically, the airport is well-equipped for easy transfers.

Shuttle Services: Shuttle buses and trains connect terminals at Kansai International Airport.

5. Airport Facilities:

Lounges: Both airports offer lounges for various airlines, providing amenities and a comfortable space for travelers.

Duty-Free Shopping: Explore duty-free shops for Japanese products, souvenirs, and luxury goods.

Restaurants: Enjoy a variety of dining options, including traditional Japanese cuisine and international flavors.

Wi-Fi Access: Free Wi-Fi is available throughout the airports.

6. Practical Tips:
Currency Exchange: Currency exchange services are available at both airports.
Baggage Services: Facilities for luggage storage and delivery services are accessible for travelers.
Information Desks: Seek assistance from information desks for any queries or travel-related information.

While Kyoto itself doesn't have an airport, navigating through Kansai International Airport or Osaka Itami Airport seamlessly connects you to the cultural heart of Japan. Plan your journey well, utilize the efficient transportation options, and make the most of the airport facilities to ensure a smooth transition to Kyoto's enchanting landscapes and historic sites. Safe travels!

Osaka Airport Guide

Osaka is served by two main airports, Kansai International Airport (KIX) and Osaka Itami Airport (ITM), each offering distinct services and connectivity. Whether you're flying internationally or domestically, here's your guide to navigating these airports in the culinary capital of Japan:

1. Kansai International Airport (KIX):
Location: Situated on an artificial island in Osaka Bay, approximately 50 minutes from central Osaka.

Access to Osaka: The JR Haruka Limited Express offers a direct connection to major Osaka stations, including Shin-Osaka and Tennoji.

Terminals: Kansai Airport has two terminals – Terminal 1 (mostly international flights) and Terminal 2 (domestic flights).

Services: Enjoy duty-free shopping, lounges, and multilingual assistance.

2. Osaka Itami Airport (ITM):
Location: Located in Itami, about 30 minutes from central Osaka.

Access to Osaka: The Osaka Monorail and Hankyu Railway provide convenient links to various parts of Osaka.

Terminals: Osaka Itami primarily handles domestic flights.

Services: Offers lounges, shopping, and dining options for domestic travelers.

3. Transportation Options from Airports:
From Kansai International Airport (KIX):

JR Haruka Limited Express: Direct train to major Osaka stations, including Shin-Osaka and Tennoji.

Nankai Railway: Train to Namba Station in Osaka, with connections to other lines.

Limousine Buses: Direct bus services to Osaka's major districts.

From Osaka Itami Airport (ITM):

Osaka Monorail and Hankyu Railway: Convenient monorail and train options connecting to various parts of Osaka.

Taxis: Taxis are readily available for direct transfers to your destination.

4. Domestic Transfers:

Connecting Flights: If transferring domestically at Osaka Itami Airport, the airport is designed for efficient connections.

Shuttle Services: Shuttle buses and trains connect terminals at Kansai International Airport.

5. Airport Facilities:

Lounges: Both airports offer lounges catering to various airlines, providing amenities and relaxation for travelers.

Duty-Free Shopping: Explore duty-free shops for Japanese products, souvenirs, and luxury goods.

Restaurants: Savor a variety of dining options, from traditional Japanese dishes to international cuisine.

Wi-Fi Access: Enjoy free Wi-Fi throughout the airports.

6. Practical Tips:

Currency Exchange: Currency exchange services are available at both airports.

Baggage Services: Facilities for luggage storage and delivery services are accessible for travelers.

Information Desks: Seek assistance from information desks for any queries or travel-related information.

Navigating Osaka's airports ensures a smooth transition to the culinary delights and vibrant energy of the city. Whether you're immersing yourself in the international atmosphere of Kansai International Airport or connecting seamlessly through Osaka Itami Airport, your journey to the culinary capital of Japan begins with a well-planned and informed airport experience. Safe travels!

Navigating Public Transport

Public transportation in Japan is renowned for its efficiency, cleanliness, and punctuality. Whether you're exploring Tokyo, Kyoto, Osaka, or other cities, understanding the public transport system is key to unlocking the full experience of this fascinating country. Here's your essential guide to navigating Japan's public transport:

1. Rail Network:
    Shinkansen (Bullet Trains): High-speed trains connect major cities. Purchase tickets or use JR Pass for cost-effective travel.
    JR Lines: Japan Railways operates extensive lines, including the Yamanote Line in Tokyo and the Osaka Loop Line.

Private Railways: Various private rail companies cover specific regions. ICOCA and Suica cards work on most rail networks.

2. Subways and Metro:
Tokyo Metro: Tokyo's subway system is well-connected. Suica or Pasmo cards simplify fare payments.

Osaka Metro: Efficient subway lines cover Osaka and neighboring cities.

Kyoto Municipal Subway: Two lines serve Kyoto, with convenient connections to buses.

3. Buses:
City Buses: Municipal buses operate in urban areas, with fixed routes and fares.

Long-Distance Buses: Connect cities and rural areas. Comfortable highway buses are cost-effective for intercity travel.

4. Taxis:
Availability: Taxis are readily available but are relatively expensive compared to other options.

Taxi Apps: Consider using taxi-hailing apps for convenience and smoother transactions.

5. Airport Transportation:
Narita Express (N'EX): Direct train from Narita Airport to Tokyo and other major stations.

Kansai Airport Express: Haruka Limited Express connects Kansai Airport to Osaka and Kyoto.

Airport Limousine Buses: Convenient bus services connect airports to major city centers.

6. IC Cards:
Suica, Pasmo, ICOCA: These contactless smart cards can be used for trains, subways, buses, and even purchases at vending machines and convenience stores.

Rechargeable: Easily rechargeable at stations, they provide a hassle-free way to pay for transportation.

7. Timeliness:
Punctuality: Public transport in Japan is renowned for its punctuality. Timetables are strictly adhered to.

Real-Time Information: Many stations provide real-time information on train arrivals and departures.

8. Signage and Maps:
English Signage: Major stations and tourist areas have English signs. Station staff often speak English.

Interactive Maps: Utilize interactive station maps and navigation apps for easy route planning.

9. Cultural Etiquette:
Queuing: Japanese people value orderly queues. Wait your turn for buses and trains.

Priority Seats: Offer priority seats to elderly, disabled, and pregnant passengers.

10. Apps and Websites:
HyperDia: Plan your train journeys with this comprehensive online timetable and route search tool.

Google Maps: Reliable for navigating public transport routes, including trains, buses, and walking directions.

11. Accessibility:
Barrier-Free Stations: Many stations are equipped with elevators and ramps for accessibility.
Accessible Taxis: Some areas offer accessible taxis for passengers with mobility challenges.

Embracing Japan's public transport system allows you to seamlessly explore the country's vibrant cities and scenic landscapes. Whether you're zipping between bustling districts on the subway or enjoying the picturesque journey on a Shinkansen, efficient public transportation is an integral part of your Japanese adventure.

Airport

Chapter 3: Accommodation

Japan offers a diverse range of accommodation options catering to various preferences and budgets. Whether you prefer the luxury of a traditional ryokan or the convenience of modern hotels, here's a guide to finding accommodation that suits your needs:

1. Hotels:
   Business Hotels: Budget-friendly and commonly found in urban areas. They offer essential amenities for a comfortable stay.
   Luxury Hotels: Japan boasts high-end accommodations with luxurious amenities, often featuring stunning views and impeccable service.
   Chain Hotels: International and local chains provide standardized services across different cities.

2. Ryokans:
   Traditional Japanese Inns: Ryokans offer a unique cultural experience, featuring tatami mat rooms, futons, and onsen (hot spring) facilities.
   Luxury Ryokans: Some ryokans cater to upscale travelers, providing exquisite kaiseki meals and exclusive services.

3. Capsule Hotels:
Compact Accommodation: Capsule hotels are known for their small pods containing a bed and basic amenities. Ideal for solo travelers on a budget.
Modern Amenities: Despite the small space, capsule hotels often offer communal spaces, showers, and sometimes even saunas.

4. Guesthouses and Hostels:
Budget-Friendly Options: Guesthouses and hostels provide affordable accommodation with shared facilities.
Social Atmosphere: Ideal for solo travelers looking to meet fellow adventurers.

5. Airbnb:
Private Rentals: Airbnb offers a range of options, from entire apartments to shared rooms, providing a local living experience.
Various Locations: Available in major cities and even in more remote areas for a unique perspective.

6. Business Ryokans:
Combining Comfort and Tradition: These accommodations blend the efficiency of business hotels with some traditional elements, offering a comfortable stay.

7. Love Hotels:
Themed Rooms: Love hotels, primarily for couples, offer themed rooms with unique designs and features.

Privacy: Discreet and often booked by the hour, they provide a level of privacy not typically found in standard hotels.

8. Temple Stays:
   Cultural Immersion: Some temples offer lodgings, providing a unique opportunity to experience Buddhist practices and traditions.
   Simple Accommodations: Temple stays usually offer simple rooms and vegetarian meals.

9. Booking Platforms:
   Online Reservations: Use platforms like Booking.com, Agoda, or Expedia to find and reserve accommodations.
   Official Websites: Check the official websites of hotels or ryokans for direct bookings and potential discounts.

10. Location Considerations:
    Proximity to Transportation: Choose accommodation near major train stations or subway lines for convenience.
    Neighborhood Atmosphere: Consider staying in neighborhoods that align with your preferences, whether bustling urban districts or quieter residential areas.

11. Japanese Inn Selections:
    Jalan and Rakuten Travel: These platforms offer a selection of ryokans and traditional inns for a more authentic experience.

Japan's accommodation options cater to a wide range of preferences, ensuring that you'll find a place that suits your needs and enhances your overall travel experience. Whether you seek the tranquility of a ryokan, the convenience of a business hotel, or the social atmosphere of a hostel, Japan's diverse lodging choices ensure a comfortable and memorable stay.

Types of Accommodation in Tokyo

Tokyo, as a bustling metropolis, offers a wide range of accommodation options to suit various preferences and budgets. Whether you're seeking traditional Japanese hospitality or modern amenities, Tokyo has it all. Here are some types of accommodation you can find in Tokyo:

1. Hotels:
    Luxury Hotels: Tokyo boasts internationally renowned luxury hotels with top-notch amenities, impeccable service, and stunning city views.
    Business Hotels: Found throughout the city, these hotels provide comfort and essential amenities, catering to business and leisure travelers alike.

2. Ryokans:

Traditional Japanese Inns: Experience Japanese hospitality with tatami mat rooms, futons, and often an onsen (hot spring) facility. Some ryokans in Tokyo offer a blend of traditional and modern elements.

3. Capsule Hotels:

Compact Accommodation: Capsule hotels provide a unique and efficient space for solo travelers. They offer a bed in a small pod with shared facilities.

4. Boutique Hotels:

Chic and Unique: Boutique hotels in Tokyo focus on individualized and stylish designs, providing a more intimate and personalized experience.

5. Guesthouses and Hostels:

Budget-Friendly Options: Tokyo has a variety of guesthouses and hostels offering shared dormitories or private rooms. Ideal for budget-conscious and solo travelers.

6. Airbnb and Vacation Rentals:

Local Living Experience: Private rentals, including apartments and houses, allow visitors to experience life like a local. Airbnb options are available in different neighborhoods across Tokyo.

7. Business Ryokans:

Combining Tradition and Efficiency: Some accommodations combine the efficiency of business hotels with traditional Japanese elements, offering a unique stay.

8. Love Hotels:
Themed Rooms: Love hotels, often found in entertainment districts, offer themed rooms and a level of privacy not typical in standard hotels.

9. Serviced Apartments:
Long-Term Stays: Ideal for extended stays, serviced apartments provide a home-like environment with kitchen facilities and additional living space.

10. Internet Cafes and Manga Cafes:
Budget Accommodation: These establishments offer private booths or small rooms for short stays, often with internet access, making them a budget-friendly option.

11. Luxury Ryokans in Tokyo:
Exquisite Experience: While ryokans are more prevalent in other regions, Tokyo does have luxury ryokans that offer traditional hospitality with a touch of elegance.

12. Temple Stays:
Cultural Immersion: Some temples in Tokyo offer accommodations, providing a unique opportunity to experience Buddhist practices and traditions in the heart of the city.

13. Family-Friendly Accommodations:
    Hotels with Family Rooms: Many hotels in Tokyo cater to families, offering spacious rooms and family-friendly amenities.

14. Pet-Friendly Accommodations:
    Pet-Friendly Hotels: Some hotels in Tokyo are pet-friendly, allowing guests to bring their furry companions along.

Whether you're looking for the opulence of a luxury hotel, the cultural immersion of a ryokan, or the budget-friendly atmosphere of a hostel, Tokyo's diverse accommodations cater to a wide range of preferences. Consider the location, amenities, and unique features to find the perfect place for your stay in this dynamic city.

Types of Accommodation Kyoto

Kyoto, with its rich history and cultural significance, offers a variety of accommodation options that reflect the city's charm. From traditional ryokans to modern hotels, Kyoto provides a unique blend of heritage and comfort. Here are some types of accommodation you can find in Kyoto:

1. Ryokans:
Traditional Japanese Inns: Kyoto is known for its exquisite ryokans, offering tatami mat rooms, futons, kaiseki meals, and onsen baths. Some are located in scenic areas like Gion and Higashiyama.

2. Machiya Stays:
Historic Townhouses: Experience Kyoto's traditional architecture by staying in a machiya, a traditional wooden townhouse. These accommodations provide a glimpse into the city's past.

3. Hotels:
Luxury Hotels: Kyoto hosts luxurious hotels with a blend of modern amenities and traditional aesthetics. Some are nestled in serene gardens, providing an oasis in the heart of the city.

Boutique Hotels: Kyoto features boutique hotels with unique designs, often reflecting the city's cultural and artistic heritage.

4. Guesthouses and Hostels:
Budget-Friendly Options: Guesthouses and hostels offer affordable stays, with shared dormitories or private rooms. They are excellent choices for solo and budget travelers.

5. Airbnb and Vacation Rentals:
Local Living Experience: Explore Kyoto like a local by staying in private rentals, such as apartments or machiyas, available on platforms like Airbnb.

6. Shukubo (Temple Lodgings):
   Cultural Immersion: Temples in Kyoto offer shukubo, allowing guests to experience a monk's lifestyle. Some temples provide vegetarian meals and opportunities to participate in meditation.

7. Business Hotels:
   Convenient and Comfortable: Kyoto has business hotels that offer essential amenities and are conveniently located near transportation hubs.

8. Capsule Hotels:
   Efficient and Compact: While less common in Kyoto, there are capsule hotels providing a unique and space-efficient accommodation option.

9. Traditional Townhouse Rentals:
   Private Residences: Some companies offer the rental of entire traditional townhouses, providing an exclusive and immersive experience.

10. Family-Friendly Accommodations:
    Hotels with Family Rooms: Many hotels in Kyoto cater to families, offering larger rooms and family-friendly amenities.

11. Pet-Friendly Accommodations:
    Pet-Friendly Hotels: While limited, some accommodations in Kyoto are pet-friendly, allowing guests to bring their pets along.

12. Internet Cafes and Manga Cafes:
Budget Stays: Some internet cafes in Kyoto offer private booths for short-term stays, providing a unique and budget-friendly option.

13. Luxury Ryokans in Kyoto:
Elegance and Tradition: Kyoto boasts high-end ryokans, offering a luxurious experience with traditional elements, exquisite kaiseki meals, and impeccable service.

Whether you seek the tranquility of a traditional ryokan, the historical ambiance of a machiya, or the convenience of a modern hotel, Kyoto's diverse accommodations provide an opportunity to immerse yourself in the city's timeless beauty and cultural heritage. Consider the location and unique features to find the perfect place for your stay in this enchanting city.

Types of Accommodation in Osaka

Osaka, known for its vibrant energy and culinary delights, offers a variety of accommodation options catering to different preferences and budgets. From modern hotels to traditional ryokans, here are some types of accommodation you can find in Osaka:

1. Hotels:
Business Hotels: Convenient and often budget-friendly, catering to business travelers and tourists alike.

Luxury Hotels: Osaka hosts upscale hotels with modern amenities, exquisite dining, and often stunning views of the cityscape.

2. Ryokans:
Traditional Japanese Inns: While not as prevalent as in other cities, Osaka has ryokans offering a blend of traditional hospitality and modern comforts.

3. Capsule Hotels:
Compact Accommodation: Capsule hotels provide a unique and efficient space, ideal for solo travelers looking for a budget-friendly option.

4. Guesthouses and Hostels:
Budget-Friendly Options: Osaka has a range of guesthouses and hostels, perfect for solo travelers or those on a budget.

5. Airbnb and Vacation Rentals:
Local Living Experience: Private rentals, including apartments and houses, offer a chance to experience local life in Osaka.

6. Love Hotels:
Themed Rooms: Love hotels, found in entertainment districts, offer themed rooms and a level of privacy not typical in standard hotels.

7. Business Ryokans:
Combining Tradition and Efficiency: Some accommodations in Osaka blend traditional Japanese elements with the efficiency of business hotels.

8. Internet Cafes and Manga Cafes:
Budget Stays: Some internet cafes in Osaka offer private booths for short-term stays, providing a unique and budget-friendly option.

9. Luxury Ryokans in Osaka:
Elegance and Tradition: While less common, Osaka has high-end ryokans offering traditional experiences with luxurious amenities.

10. Family-Friendly Accommodations:
Hotels with Family Rooms: Many hotels in Osaka cater to families, offering larger rooms and family-friendly amenities.

11. Pet-Friendly Accommodations:
Pet-Friendly Hotels: Limited but available, some accommodations in Osaka allow guests to bring their pets along.

12. Short Stay Apartments:
Extended Stays: Some serviced apartments provide more extended stay options, offering kitchen facilities and additional living space.

13. Temples with Accommodations:
Cultural Immersion: A few temples in Osaka offer lodgings, allowing guests to experience Buddhist practices and traditions.

14. Minshuku:
Local Guesthouses: Similar to ryokans, minshuku are smaller guesthouses offering a more intimate and local experience.

Whether you're seeking the convenience of a business hotel, the unique experience of a love hotel, or the traditional charm of a ryokan, Osaka's diverse accommodations cater to a wide range of preferences. Consider the location, amenities, and unique features to find the perfect place for your stay in this dynamic and lively city.

Recommended Hotels in Tokyo

Tokyo offers a plethora of accommodation options, from luxurious hotels to unique boutique stays. Here are some recommended hotels that combine comfort with a touch of Japanese culture:

1. Aman Tokyo:
   Location: Otemachi, near the Imperial Palace.
   Highlights: Aman Tokyo exudes luxury with spacious rooms, panoramic city views, and a serene atmosphere. The hotel seamlessly blends traditional Japanese aesthetics with modern design.

2. Andaz Tokyo Toranomon Hills:
   Location: Toranomon Hills, Minato-ku.
   Highlights: This upscale hotel features contemporary design, spacious rooms, and a rooftop bar with stunning views of Tokyo Tower. The Andaz Tokyo embraces a modern and stylish ambiance.

3. Hoshinoya Tokyo:
Location: Otemachi, near Tokyo Station.
Highlights: A unique blend of traditional ryokan elements and modern luxury. Hoshinoya Tokyo offers spacious rooms with tatami mat floors, providing an authentic yet luxurious Japanese experience.

4. Mandarin Oriental Tokyo:
Location: Nihonbashi, Chuo-ku.
Highlights: Overlooking Tokyo's skyline, this five-star hotel boasts elegant rooms, exceptional dining, and a spa with panoramic city views. The Mandarin Oriental Tokyo is synonymous with sophistication.

5. Park Hyatt Tokyo:
Location: Shinjuku.
Highlights: Familiar to fans of the movie "Lost in Translation," the Park Hyatt Tokyo offers luxurious rooms, world-class dining, and breathtaking views of the city. The ambiance is chic and contemporary.

6. Hotel Ryumeikan Ochanomizu Honten:
Location: Ochanomizu, Bunkyo-ku.
Highlights: A blend of modernity and traditional elements, this hotel is close to Akihabara and offers comfortable rooms with Japanese-inspired design. The location is convenient for exploring Tokyo's attractions.

7. The Prince Gallery Tokyo Kioicho:
   Location: Kioicho, Chiyoda-ku.
   Highlights: Situated in a skyscraper, this luxury hotel boasts spacious rooms, contemporary design, and stunning views of the city. The Prince Gallery Tokyo Kioicho offers a sophisticated stay.

8. Trunk Hotel:
   Location: Shibuya.
   Highlights: A boutique hotel with a focus on sustainability and design, Trunk Hotel offers stylish rooms, a trendy atmosphere, and a commitment to eco-friendly practices.

9. Akihabara Bay Hotel:
   Location: Akihabara.
   Highlights: For a unique and budget-friendly experience, Akihabara Bay Hotel provides capsule-style accommodations with modern amenities, perfect for solo travelers.

10. Hotel Niwa Tokyo:
    Location: Suidobashi, Bunkyo-ku.
    Highlights: Combining modern comfort with a touch of nature, Hotel Niwa Tokyo features a garden courtyard and contemporary rooms. The hotel provides a peaceful retreat in the heart of the city.

Remember to consider your preferences, budget, and the location of your desired activities when choosing a hotel in Tokyo. These recommendations offer a range of options to suit various tastes, ensuring a comfortable and culturally rich stay in Japan's capital.

Recommended Hotels in Kyoto

Kyoto, with its historical charm, offers a range of accommodations blending traditional elements with modern comforts. Here are some recommended hotels that provide a unique and comfortable stay in this cultural capital:

1. The Ritz-Carlton Kyoto:
   Location: Kamogawa Nijo-Ohashi Hotori, Nakagyo-ku.
   Highlights: Overlooking the Kamogawa River, The Ritz-Carlton Kyoto combines luxury with a traditional aesthetic. Experience spacious rooms, fine dining, and impeccable service.

2. Hoshinoya Kyoto:
   Location: Arashiyama, Nishikyo-ku.
   Highlights: Nestled by the Oi River, Hoshinoya Kyoto is a luxury ryokan offering a serene atmosphere. Traditional architecture, tatami mat rooms, and kaiseki dining provide an authentic Japanese experience.

3. Hotel The Celestine Kyoto Gion:
Location: Gion, Higashiyama-ku.
Highlights: Situated in the historic Gion district, this boutique hotel features elegant design, modern amenities, and a tranquil ambiance. It provides easy access to Kyoto's cultural attractions.

4. Four Seasons Hotel Kyoto:
Location: Seiwadai, Higashiyama-ku.
Highlights: Surrounded by gardens, the Four Seasons Hotel Kyoto offers luxurious rooms, a spa, and multiple dining options. Its architecture reflects Kyoto's traditional machiya townhouses.

5. Hyatt Regency Kyoto:
Location: Higashiyama Shichijo, Higashiyama-ku.
Highlights: Blending contemporary design with Japanese aesthetics, the Hyatt Regency Kyoto provides comfortable rooms, a serene garden, and proximity to cultural landmarks.

6. Suiran, a Luxury Collection Hotel Kyoto:
Location: Saga-Tenryuji, Ukyo-ku.
Highlights: Set along the Hozugawa River, Suiran offers a tranquil retreat with modern amenities. The hotel features traditional tea houses, a spa, and beautiful garden views.

7. Gion Hatanaka:
Location: Gion, Higashiyama-ku.
Highlights: A ryokan in the heart of Gion, Gion Hatanaka provides an authentic experience with tatami mat rooms, yukata attire, and kaiseki dining.

8. The Westin Miyako Kyoto:
Location: Sanjo, Sakyoku.
Highlights: Nestled in a scenic hillside, The Westin Miyako Kyoto offers a blend of Western comfort and Japanese elegance. The expansive grounds include gardens and a historic aqueduct.

9. Kyoto Yura Hotel MGallery:
Location: Sanjo Karasuma, Nakagyo-ku.
Highlights: A contemporary hotel with a touch of nostalgia, Kyoto Yura Hotel embraces the city's cultural heritage while providing modern conveniences.

10. Guest House Rakuza:
Location: Nijojocho, Nakagyo-ku.
Highlights: For a more budget-friendly and communal experience, Guest House Rakuza offers shared dormitories and private rooms with a traditional Japanese design.

Remember to consider the location in relation to the attractions you plan to visit and the experience you desire when selecting a hotel in Kyoto. These recommendations offer a mix of luxury, traditional charm, and unique settings for a memorable stay in the cultural heart of Japan.

Recommended Hotels in Osaka

Osaka, a vibrant city known for its culinary scene and lively atmosphere, offers a range of accommodations. Here are some recommended hotels that provide a comfortable and convenient stay in this dynamic metropolis:

1. InterContinental Osaka:
   Location: Kita-ku, Umeda.
   Highlights: Situated in the heart of Umeda, InterContinental Osaka offers luxurious rooms, panoramic city views, and easy access to shopping and dining.

2. The St. Regis Osaka:
   Location: Chuo-ku, Midosuji.
   Highlights: A five-star hotel in the prestigious Midosuji district, The St. Regis Osaka boasts elegant rooms, personalized service, and proximity to Osaka's upscale shopping areas.

3. Hotel Hankyu International:
   Location: Kita-ku, Umeda.
   Highlights: Located near Umeda Station, this hotel combines modern luxury with Japanese hospitality. Spacious rooms and multiple dining options make it a comfortable choice.

4. Swissotel Nankai Osaka:
   Location: Chuo-ku, Namba.
   Highlights: Overlooking Namba Parks, Swissotel Nankai Osaka provides contemporary rooms, diverse dining choices, and a central location close to shopping and entertainment.

5. Osaka Marriott Miyako Hotel:
   Location: Abeno-ku, Tennoji.
   Highlights: Situated in the Abeno Harukas building, the Osaka Marriott Miyako Hotel offers breathtaking city views, modern amenities, and easy access to Tennoji attractions.

6. Hotel New Otani Osaka:
   Location: Chuo-ku, Osaka Castle.
   Highlights: With a view of Osaka Castle, this hotel combines comfort with history. Spacious rooms, multiple dining options, and a serene garden contribute to a pleasant stay.

7. Cross Hotel Osaka:
Location: Chuo-ku, Shinsaibashi.
Highlights: Nestled in the lively Shinsaibashi district, Cross Hotel Osaka provides stylish rooms, a rooftop bar, and proximity to shopping and entertainment.

8. Hotel Granvia Osaka:
Location: Kita-ku, Umeda.
Highlights: Connected to Osaka Station, Hotel Granvia Osaka offers convenience and comfort with modern amenities and easy access to transportation.

9. Moxy Osaka Honmachi:
Location: Chuo-ku, Honmachi.
Highlights: A contemporary and stylish option, Moxy Osaka Honmachi provides a vibrant atmosphere, modern design, and a central location.

10. Osaka Bay Tower Hotel:
Location: Suminoe-ku, Osaka Bay.
Highlights: Offering panoramic views of Osaka Bay, this hotel provides a unique experience. Spacious rooms, multiple dining options, and proximity to Osaka Aquarium Kaiyukan make it a notable choice.

Remember to consider the location in relation to your planned activities and the experience you desire when choosing a hotel in Osaka. Whether you prefer the bustling atmosphere of Namba or the modern elegance of Umeda, these recommendations offer a range of options for a delightful stay in Osaka.

Budget-Friendly Options

For those seeking economical options without compromising comfort, Tokyo, Kyoto, and Osaka offer a variety of budget-friendly accommodations. Here are some recommendations in each city:

Tokyo:

1. K's House Tokyo Oasis:
   Location: Asakusa.
   Highlights: A hostel with dormitory-style rooms and private options, K's House Tokyo Oasis is known for its friendly atmosphere and proximity to Asakusa's cultural attractions.

2. Sakura Hotel Ikebukuro:
   Location: Ikebukuro.
   Highlights: Affordable private and dormitory rooms, multicultural staff, and a convenient location near Ikebukuro Station make Sakura Hotel Ikebukuro a popular choice.

3. Capsule Hotel Asakusa Riverside:
   Location: Asakusa.
   Highlights: For a unique experience, this capsule hotel offers compact yet comfortable sleeping pods,

communal areas, and an affordable stay in the historic Asakusa district.

Kyoto:

1. Piece Hostel Kyoto:
Location: Kawaramachi.
Highlights: Centrally located in the Gion area, Piece Hostel Kyoto provides modern dormitories and private rooms, fostering a social environment for travelers.

2. Kyoto Hana Hostel:
Location: Gion.
Highlights: With a charming traditional design, Kyoto Hana Hostel offers budget-friendly dormitory and private rooms, just a short walk from Gion's historic streets.

3. The Millennials Kyoto:
Location: Shijo-Karasuma.
Highlights: A unique concept combining capsule-style accommodation with communal spaces, The Millennials Kyoto offers a modern and affordable stay in the city center.

Osaka:

1. J-Hoppers Osaka Guesthouse:
Location: Tennoji.
Highlights: Known for its friendly atmosphere and communal spaces, J-Hoppers Osaka Guesthouse

provides budget-friendly dormitories and private rooms in the vibrant Tennoji area.

2. Hotel Mikado:
 Location: Namba.
 Highlights: Conveniently located in Namba, Hotel Mikado offers affordable private and dormitory rooms, making it a suitable choice for budget-conscious travelers.

3. Hostel Enisia Namba:
 Location: Namba.
 Highlights: Budget-friendly dormitory rooms and a sociable atmosphere make Hostel Enisia Namba an excellent option for those exploring Osaka's entertainment district.

These budget-friendly accommodations provide a mix of affordability, convenience, and often a chance to meet fellow travelers. Whether you're exploring the historic streets of Kyoto, the bustling neighborhoods of Tokyo, or the vibrant cityscape of Osaka, these options offer comfort without breaking the bank.

Chapter 4: Exploring Tokyo

Tokyo, the pulsating heart of Japan, seamlessly weaves together a rich tapestry of tradition and modernity. As you embark on your exploration of this vibrant metropolis, be prepared for a sensory journey that encapsulates the essence of Japan's past, present, and future.

1. Historical Enclaves:
   Tokyo's historical districts offer a glimpse into Japan's cultural heritage. Start with Asakusa, where the iconic Senso-ji Temple stands, surrounded by traditional shops on Nakamise Street. Immerse yourself in the serene beauty of Meiji Shrine in Shibuya, nestled within a lush forest, providing a tranquil escape from the urban hustle.

2. Modern Marvels:
   Tokyo's skyline is a testament to its innovation and progress. The Tokyo Skytree, towering over Sumida, offers breathtaking panoramic views of the city. In the upscale district of Roppongi, the Mori Art Museum and Tokyo City View provide a cultural and artistic perspective from above.

3. Culinary Odyssey:
Tokyo's culinary scene is a kaleidoscope of flavors. Dive into the bustling Tsukiji Outer Market for a seafood extravaganza, or wander through the narrow alleys of Yurakucho to savor yakitori grilled to perfection. For a unique experience, explore the themed cafes in Akihabara or sip matcha in a traditional tea house in Ueno.

4. Akihabara: Electric Town Extravaganza:
Akihabara, synonymous with otaku culture and electronics, is a haven for tech enthusiasts and anime/manga lovers. Explore the myriad of electronic shops, anime stores, and themed cafes that line the streets. Dive into the vibrant subcultures that define this district, from gaming centers to anime mega-stores.

5. Shinjuku: A Dynamic Hub:
Shinjuku is a microcosm of Tokyo's dynamism. Wander through Shinjuku Gyoen National Garden, a serene oasis amidst the urban chaos. Explore the buzzing streets around Shinjuku Station, home to diverse dining options, entertainment hubs, and the iconic Kabukicho district, Tokyo's renowned nightlife area.

6. Harajuku: Fashion and Street Culture:
Harajuku, a fashion mecca, beckons with its eclectic street style and trendy boutiques. Takeshita Street is a carnival of colors and unique fashion statements. Adjacent to this lively scene lies the tranquil Meiji

Shrine, a stark contrast that encapsulates Tokyo's ability to harmonize extremes.

7. Odaiba: Futuristic Entertainment Island:
Odaiba, a man-made island in Tokyo Bay, is a futuristic playground. Visit the life-sized Gundam statue, relax in Odaiba Seaside Park, or explore entertainment complexes like Palette Town. The Rainbow Bridge illuminates the skyline at night, adding a touch of magic to the bay area.

8. Ueno Park: Culture and Nature Coalesce:
Ueno Park is a cultural haven housing museums, a zoo, and serene cherry blossom avenues. Visit the Tokyo National Museum for a historical journey, and don't miss the seasonal beauty of cherry blossoms in spring or vibrant autumn foliage.

9. Tokyo Disneyland and DisneySea: Magic and Adventure:
For a whimsical escape, Tokyo Disneyland and DisneySea offer enchanting experiences for visitors of all ages. Immerse yourself in the magic of classic Disney attractions and explore the uniquely themed areas of DisneySea.

10. Transportation Odyssey:
Tokyo's efficient and extensive public transportation system, including the iconic JR Yamanote Line, makes exploration seamless. Dive into the labyrinth of subway stations, hop on a Shinkansen for a day trip, or cruise

along the Sumida River for a different perspective of the city.

Tokyo, with its juxtaposition of tradition and modernity, creates an unforgettable tableau for every explorer. Whether you're savoring street food in old districts, admiring futuristic architecture, or embracing the harmony of a traditional tea ceremony, Tokyo invites you into a world where past and present dance in harmony. The city's dynamic spirit, cultural depth, and innovative energy promise a journey that transcends time and leaves an indelible mark on every traveler.

Tokyo Must-Visit Attractions

Tokyo, a city where tradition and innovation harmonize, invites you to explore its myriad of must-visit attractions. From ancient temples to futuristic landmarks, here's a curated list to guide your exploration of Japan's dynamic capital:

1. Senso-ji Temple (Asakusa):
   Tokyo's oldest temple, Senso-ji, offers a spiritual journey. Pass through the iconic Thunder Gate, wander Nakamise Street's traditional stalls, and bask in the tranquility of the Main Hall and Five-story Pagoda.

2. Tokyo Skytree (Sumida):
   Soar to new heights at Tokyo Skytree, providing breathtaking panoramic views of the city. The towering

structure is an architectural marvel, and its observation decks offer an unrivaled perspective of Tokyo's skyline.
Senso-ji Temple

3. Meiji Shrine (Shibuya):
Nestled within a lush forest, Meiji Shrine in Shibuya offers a serene escape from the urban hustle. The impressive Torii Gate marks the entrance, leading to the shrine's tranquil grounds and the picturesque Inner Garden.

4. Tsukiji Outer Market and Toyosu Fish Market:
Dive into Tokyo's culinary scene at Tsukiji Outer Market for fresh seafood delicacies. While the inner market has moved to Toyosu, the outer market continues to offer a feast of sushi, sashimi, and street food.

5. Shibuya Crossing:
Witness the mesmerizing organized chaos of Shibuya Crossing, an iconic Tokyo scene. Join the flow of pedestrians as the traffic halts, capturing the dynamic energy of this bustling district.

6. Akihabara: Electric Town:
Akihabara is a tech and otaku paradise. Explore electronic shops, anime stores, and themed cafes. Dive into the vibrant subcultures that define this district, from gaming centers to anime mega-stores.

7. Odaiba:
A man-made island, Odaiba, offers a futuristic playground. Visit the life-sized Gundam statue, explore entertainment complexes like Palette Town, and enjoy the breathtaking views of Rainbow Bridge.

8. Ueno Park and Museums:
Ueno Park is a cultural hub featuring museums, a zoo, and cherry blossom-lined avenues. Visit the Tokyo National Museum, Tokyo Metropolitan Art Museum, and Ueno Zoo for a diverse experience.

9. Tokyo Disneyland and DisneySea:
Delight in the magic of Tokyo Disneyland and DisneySea. Immerse yourself in classic Disney attractions, themed areas, and enchanting entertainment for visitors of all ages.

10. Asakusa Cultural and Tourist Information Center:
Head to this architectural gem for a stunning view of Tokyo Skytree and the Asakusa district. The observation deck provides a unique perspective, and the building itself is a blend of modern design and functionality.

11. Ginza Shopping District:
Indulge in luxury and style at Ginza, Tokyo's upscale shopping district. Explore designer boutiques, department stores, and enjoy gourmet dining in this chic neighborhood.

12. Roppongi Hills (Roppongi):
Roppongi Hills is a modern complex offering shopping, dining, and cultural experiences. Visit the Mori Art Museum for contemporary art, enjoy panoramic views, and explore Tokyo's vibrant nightlife.

From the historic charm of Asakusa to the cutting-edge technology of Odaiba, Tokyo beckons with a diverse array of attractions. Whether you're drawn to traditional temples, modern skyscrapers, or the whimsical magic of Disneyland, each stop promises a unique facet of Tokyo's multifaceted allure.

Tokyo Neighborhood Highlights

Neighborhood Highlights in Tokyo: A Tapestry of Diversity

Tokyo's neighborhoods are like chapters in a captivating story, each offering a unique blend of tradition, modernity, and distinct character. Explore the highlights of key neighborhoods to truly grasp the vibrant tapestry that is Tokyo:

Asakusa:

1. Senso-ji Temple:
    Begin your journey at Senso-ji, Tokyo's oldest temple. Pass through the iconic Thunder Gate, stroll along Nakamise Street's vibrant stalls, and experience the spiritual ambiance of the Main Hall.

2. Asakusa Culture and Tourist Information Center:
Visit this architectural gem for panoramic views of Tokyo Skytree and the Asakusa district. The futuristic design and observation deck provide a modern contrast to the traditional surroundings.

3. Sumida Aquarium:
Explore the enchanting underwater world at Sumida Aquarium, located in Tokyo Skytree Town. From jellyfish exhibits to immersive displays, it offers a delightful marine experience.

Shibuya:

1. Shibuya Crossing:
Dive into the organized chaos of Shibuya Crossing, one of Tokyo's iconic scenes. Experience the rush as pedestrians cross simultaneously, creating a mesmerizing spectacle.

2. Meiji Shrine:
Find serenity in the heart of Shibuya at Meiji Shrine. The tranquil forested grounds, Torii Gate entrance, and Inner Garden provide a peaceful contrast to the bustling urban surroundings.

3. Shibuya Center Street:
Shop and dine along Shibuya Center Street, a vibrant area filled with trendy boutiques, cafes, and restaurants. Experience Tokyo's youth culture and fashion trends.

Asakusa

Shinjuku:

1. Shinjuku Gyoen National Garden:
Escape the urban hustle in Shinjuku Gyoen, a beautiful blend of traditional Japanese, English, and French garden landscapes. Cherry blossoms in spring and vibrant foliage in autumn enhance its allure.

2. Golden Gai:
Immerse yourself in Golden Gai, a district known for its narrow alleys lined with unique, tiny bars. Experience the intimate atmosphere and diverse themes of these eclectic watering holes.

3. Robot Restaurant:
Dive into the futuristic and eccentric world of Robot Restaurant in Kabukicho. Enjoy a sensory overload of neon lights, robots, and entertainment in this dazzling spectacle.

Ginza:

1. Ginza Shopping District:
Indulge in luxury and sophistication at Ginza, Tokyo's upscale shopping district. Explore designer boutiques, department stores, and relish gourmet dining experiences.

2. Kabukiza Theatre:
Witness traditional Japanese performing arts at Kabukiza Theatre. Experience the captivating art of

kabuki, a classical theater form with elaborate costumes and dramatic storytelling.

3. Tsukiji Outer Market:
Savor the freshest seafood at Tsukiji Outer Market. Indulge in sushi, sashimi, and other culinary delights as you navigate through the bustling stalls.

Akihabara:

1. Electric Town:
Akihabara, or Electric Town, is a haven for tech enthusiasts and anime/manga lovers. Explore electronic shops, anime stores, and themed cafes that define the district's vibrant subcultures.

2. Akihabara Radio Kaikan:
Discover the history of Akihabara's pop culture at Radio Kaikan. The building houses shops, exhibitions, and showcases the evolution of anime, manga, and gaming.

3. Maid Cafes:
Experience the unique culture of Akihabara with a visit to a maid cafe. Enjoy themed food and beverages served by staff in maid costumes, creating a whimsical atmosphere.

These neighborhood highlights provide a glimpse into the diverse facets of Tokyo. Whether you seek spiritual retreats, urban excitement, or cultural immersion, each district contributes to Tokyo's multifaceted charm.

Dining and Nightlife in Tokyo

Tokyo's dining scene is a gastronomic adventure, offering everything from traditional delicacies to innovative fusion cuisine. As night falls, the city transforms into a kaleidoscope of lights and lively districts. Here's a guide to experiencing the best of dining and nightlife in Tokyo:

Dining:

1. Sushi in Tsukiji or Toyosu:
   Begin your culinary journey with fresh sushi at Tsukiji Outer Market or Toyosu Fish Market. Savor a variety of nigiri, sashimi, and other seafood delights from renowned sushi establishments.

2. Ramen in Ikebukuro:
   Explore Ikebukuro's ramen street, where you'll find a plethora of ramen shops offering diverse flavors and styles. From rich tonkotsu to savory shoyu, indulge in this Japanese comfort food.

3. Yakitori in Shinjuku's Omoide Yokocho:
   Dive into the world of yakitori (grilled chicken skewers) in Omoide Yokocho, also known as "Memory

Lane." Sample various skewers paired with drinks in this atmospheric alley.
Dining

4. Izakayas in Golden Gai, Shinjuku:
Golden Gai is home to numerous tiny izakayas (Japanese pubs). Experience local camaraderie, enjoy small dishes, and try a variety of drinks in this eclectic district.

5. Kaiseki in Ginza:
Indulge in a traditional kaiseki dining experience in Ginza, Tokyo's upscale district. Savor meticulously prepared multi-course meals showcasing the beauty of Japanese culinary artistry.

Nightlife:

1. Roppongi Hills:
Begin your nightlife exploration in Roppongi Hills. Enjoy upscale bars and lounges with panoramic views of the city. Roppongi's vibrant nightlife scene caters to diverse tastes.

2. Shinjuku Ni-chome:
Explore Shinjuku Ni-chome, Tokyo's LGBTQ+ district. This area offers a lively atmosphere with a variety of bars, clubs, and entertainment venues welcoming everyone.

3. Omoide Yokocho in Shinjuku:
As night falls, Omoide Yokocho transforms into a bustling nightlife hub. Sip on drinks in tiny bars, enjoy local vibes, and immerse yourself in the energy of this nostalgic alley.

Nightlife

4. Ginza Rooftop Bars:
Elevate your nightlife experience at one of Ginza's rooftop bars. Enjoy cocktails with breathtaking views of Tokyo's illuminated skyline, creating a sophisticated and memorable evening.

5. Shibuya Entertainment District:
Shibuya boasts a diverse nightlife scene. From trendy clubs to cozy bars, explore the entertainment district for an unforgettable night out. The area around Center Street is particularly vibrant.

6. Kabukicho in Shinjuku:
Kabukicho is Tokyo's renowned entertainment and red-light district. Discover unique themed bars, experience robot shows, and explore the myriad entertainment options in this lively area.

7. Ikebukuro's Sunshine City:
Head to Ikebukuro's Sunshine City for late-night entertainment. Enjoy karaoke, visit arcades, or experience the vibrant atmosphere of Ikebukuro's entertainment complexes.

8. Tokyo Jazz Joints:
Jazz enthusiasts can explore Tokyo's intimate jazz joints in districts like Roppongi and Shinjuku. Enjoy live performances and cozy atmospheres in these hidden gems.

Chapter 5: Discovering Kyoto

Kyoto, the cultural heart of Japan, beckons with its historic temples, traditional tea houses, and enchanting gardens. Embark on a timeless journey through this city steeped in tradition and beauty:

Historical Treasures:

1. Kinkaku-ji (Golden Pavilion):
   Begin your exploration at Kinkaku-ji, a Zen Buddhist temple covered in gold leaf. The shimmering golden facade reflected in the surrounding pond creates a breathtaking scene.

2. Fushimi Inari Taisha:
   Walk through the iconic torii gates of Fushimi Inari Taisha, dedicated to the Shinto god of rice. The path leads to the mountaintop shrine, offering panoramic views and a sense of spiritual tranquility.

3. Kiyomizu-dera:
   Perched on wooden pillars, Kiyomizu-dera provides stunning views of Kyoto. The wooden terrace juts out over the hillside, offering a breathtaking perspective, especially during cherry blossom season.

4. Gion District:
   Immerse yourself in the charm of Gion, Kyoto's historic geisha district. Stroll along Hanami-koji Street,

known for its traditional machiya houses, teahouses, and the elusive geiko and maiko.

5. Arashiyama Bamboo Grove:
Explore the ethereal beauty of the Arashiyama Bamboo Grove. The towering bamboo stalks create a serene atmosphere, and nearby attractions like Iwatayama Monkey Park add to the natural allure.

Cultural Experiences:

1. Tea Ceremony in Uji:
Engage in a traditional Japanese tea ceremony in Uji, renowned for its tea culture. Experience the meticulous preparation and serene ambiance of this ancient ritual.

2. Maiko Performance in Gion Corner:
Witness the grace and artistry of maiko (apprentice geisha) in a cultural performance at Gion Corner. The show introduces traditional arts such as tea ceremony, flower arranging, and traditional dance.

3. Kimono Rental and Hanami:
Rent a kimono and stroll through the historic districts during cherry blossom season (hanami). Experience the beauty of sakura while adorned in traditional attire.

Scenic Retreats:

1. Philosopher's Path:
Wander along the Philosopher's Path, a canal-lined walkway renowned for its cherry blossoms. The scenic route takes you past temples, shrines, and serene landscapes.

2. Garden Retreats – Ryoan-ji and Tenryu-ji:
Discover the tranquility of Ryoan-ji's Zen rock garden and the lush beauty of Tenryu-ji's gardens in the Arashiyama district. These serene spaces provide a peaceful escape.

Culinary Delights:

1. Kaiseki Dining:
Indulge in kaiseki, a multi-course dining experience showcasing the essence of Kyoto's seasonal ingredients. Renowned restaurants in Gion and Higashiyama offer exquisite kaiseki meals.

2. Yudofu in Gion:
Taste yudofu (tofu hot pot) in Gion, a delicacy enjoyed in the historic district. This simple yet flavorful dish highlights Kyoto's dedication to the art of tofu.

Modern Kyoto:

1. Kyoto International Manga Museum:
   Explore the Kyoto International Manga Museum, a modern cultural institution preserving and showcasing a vast collection of manga. Visitors can freely browse and enjoy the extensive manga library.

2. Kyoto Station and Skywalk:
   Marvel at the modern architecture of Kyoto Station. Take a stroll through the Skywalk for panoramic views, and explore the station's shopping and dining options.

Practical Tips:

Public Transportation:
   Kyoto's efficient bus system and subway make it easy to navigate the city. Consider purchasing a one-day bus pass for convenience.

Bicycle Rentals:
   Explore Kyoto on two wheels by renting a bicycle. Many attractions are easily accessible by bike, providing a leisurely and eco-friendly way to discover the city.

Seasonal Considerations:
   Kyoto's beauty varies with the seasons. Visit during cherry blossom season (spring) for stunning blooms or in autumn for vibrant fall foliage.

Kyoto, with its timeless beauty and cultural richness, offers a journey into Japan's past and present. Whether you're captivated by historic temples, serene gardens, or the allure of traditional arts, Kyoto promises an unforgettable exploration of Japan's cultural heritage.

Historical Landmarks in Tokyo

Tokyo, a city known for its modernity, also holds a treasure trove of historical landmarks that offer a glimpse into its rich past. Explore these key sites that stand as testaments to Tokyo's enduring history:

1. Senso-ji Temple (Asakusa):
   Tokyo's oldest temple, Senso-ji, dates back to 628 AD. The iconic Thunder Gate, Nakamise Street with traditional stalls, and the Main Hall create a cultural and spiritual center in Asakusa.

2. Tokyo Imperial Palace:
   Discover the historical and symbolic heart of Tokyo at the Imperial Palace. Surrounded by moats and gardens, the palace grounds incorporate Edo Castle's remnants, once home to the Tokugawa shogunate.

3. Meiji Shrine (Shibuya):
   Built in 1920, Meiji Shrine is dedicated to Emperor Meiji and Empress Shoken. The tranquil forest setting in

Shibuya provides a stark contrast to the bustling urban surroundings.

4. Edo-Tokyo Museum (Ryogoku):
Immerse yourself in Tokyo's history at the Edo-Tokyo Museum. The exhibits trace the city's evolution from the Edo period to its transformation into the bustling metropolis it is today.

5. Rikugien Garden (Bunkyo):
Dating back to 1702, Rikugien is one of Tokyo's most beautiful Japanese gardens. The landscaped scenery and traditional teahouses transport visitors to the elegance of the Edo period.

6. Koishikawa Korakuen Garden (Bunkyo):
Established in the 17th century, Koishikawa Korakuen is another exquisite garden. Its design reflects Chinese and Japanese influences, creating a serene oasis in the heart of Tokyo.

7. Zojo-ji Temple (Minato):
Founded in 1393, Zojo-ji is a Buddhist temple with ties to the Tokugawa shogunate. The temple's main hall and Daimon Gate are prominent historical structures in the Shiba district.

8. Ueno Toshogu Shrine (Ueno Park):
Modeled after Nikko Toshogu, this shrine in Ueno Park honors Tokugawa Ieyasu, the founder of the Tokugawa shogunate. The vibrant red and gold architecture adds a touch of historical grandeur to the park.

9. Tokyo National Museum (Ueno):
Established in 1872, the Tokyo National Museum is Japan's oldest and largest museum. Its extensive collection showcases traditional art, crafts, and archaeological artifacts.

10. Yushima Seido Confucian Temple (Bunkyo):
Built in 1690, Yushima Seido is a Confucian temple dedicated to Confucius. The serene courtyard and historic halls make it a peaceful retreat in Bunkyo.

11. Kyu Shiba Rikyu Garden (Minato):
Originally constructed in the 17th century, Kyu Shiba Rikyu is a traditional Japanese garden with a pond and teahouse. The garden provides a serene escape in the bustling urban landscape.

These historical landmarks weave a narrative of Tokyo's journey through centuries, from ancient temples to Edo-era remnants. Each site offers a unique perspective on the city's cultural and architectural heritage, inviting visitors to explore Tokyo beyond its contemporary façade.

Kyoto Traditional Culture Experiences

Kyoto, deeply rooted in Japan's cultural heritage, invites you to step back in time and engage in immersive traditional experiences. From tea ceremonies to kimono-wearing adventures, explore the rich tapestry of Kyoto's cultural offerings:

1. Tea Ceremony Experience:
   Participate in a traditional Japanese tea ceremony, known as "chanoyu" or "sadō." Engage in the art of tea preparation, savor matcha (green tea), and appreciate the serene atmosphere of tea houses in Kyoto's historic districts.

2. Kimono Rental and Stroll:
   Embrace the elegance of Kyoto by renting a kimono. Choose from a variety of styles and colors, and stroll through historic districts like Gion or Higashiyama. Capture the essence of traditional Japan in your attire.

3. Maiko and Geisha Experiences:
   Experience the world of maiko (apprentice geisha) in Kyoto. Attend a maiko performance in Gion Corner, where traditional arts like dance and music are showcased. Some experiences also offer the opportunity to interact with maiko.

4. Calligraphy Workshops:
Unleash your creativity with a calligraphy workshop. Learn the art of "shodō" (Japanese calligraphy) by practicing brushstrokes and creating your own piece of art under the guidance of a skilled instructor.

5. Traditional Kaiseki Dining:
Indulge in a kaiseki dining experience, a multi-course meal that embodies Kyoto's culinary artistry. Savor seasonal ingredients prepared with precision and presented in a way that is both visually stunning and delicious.

6. Ikebana (Flower Arrangement) Classes:
Explore the art of ikebana, traditional Japanese flower arrangement. Join a workshop to learn the principles of harmony and balance while creating your own floral masterpiece.

7. Noh or Kabuki Theater Performances:
Attend a traditional Noh or Kabuki theater performance for a taste of classical Japanese performing arts. These centuries-old art forms showcase elaborate costumes, refined movements, and historical narratives.

8. Pottery and Ceramic Workshops:
Get your hands dirty in a pottery or ceramic workshop. Kyoto has a rich tradition of craftsmanship, and you can try your hand at creating your own pottery under the guidance of skilled artisans.

9. Visit Traditional Machiya Houses:

Explore Kyoto's well-preserved machiya houses, traditional wooden townhouses. Some offer guided tours, providing insights into the architectural and cultural aspects of these historic residences.

10. Garden Tours and Tea in Gion:

Join guided garden tours in Gion, discovering the hidden beauty of traditional Japanese gardens. Some experiences include tea ceremonies, allowing you to enjoy matcha in a tranquil garden setting.

11. Shinise Shopping in Kyoto:

Visit "shinise," longstanding traditional shops, where you can purchase local crafts, sweets, and goods. Kyoto's historic districts are home to many of these time-honored establishments.

12. Zen Meditation Sessions:

Delve into the world of Zen Buddhism with meditation sessions. Some temples in Kyoto offer guided meditation experiences, providing a moment of reflection and tranquility.

Whether you're donning a kimono, sipping matcha, or creating your own piece of art, Kyoto's traditional culture experiences promise an authentic and enriching journey into Japan's cultural heritage. Each activity offers a unique window into the beauty and grace that define Kyoto's centuries-old traditions.

Culinary Delights within Kyoto

Kyoto, a city celebrated for its rich cultural heritage, also boasts a diverse and delectable culinary scene. From traditional kaiseki meals to local street food, immerse yourself in Kyoto's culinary tapestry:

1. Kaiseki Dining:
   Description: Indulge in the artistry of kaiseki, a multi-course dining experience that highlights Kyoto's seasonal ingredients. Each course is meticulously prepared to create a harmonious and visually stunning meal.
   Recommended Places: Ganko Sushi, Kikunoi, Gion Nanba

2. Yudofu (Tofu Hot Pot):
   Description: Savor the simplicity of yudofu, a hot pot dish featuring tofu as the main ingredient. Enjoy the delicate flavors of tofu served with dipping sauces and complemented by seasonal vegetables.
   Recommended Places: Tousuiro, Shoraian, Izuu

3. Kyo-ryori (Kyoto Cuisine):
   Description: Explore the nuances of Kyo-ryori, Kyoto's traditional cuisine. Delight in dishes that showcase local

flavors, such as pickled vegetables, Kyoto-style sushi, and elegant presentations.

Recommended Places: Ganko Sushi, Hyotei, Kikunoi

4. Obanzai:

Description: Obanzai refers to Kyoto's home-style cooking, featuring a variety of small dishes that highlight local and seasonal ingredients. It's a celebration of the region's culinary heritage.

Recommended Places: Ganko Sushi, Kappa Sushi, Izuu

5. Matcha Sweets:

Description: Kyoto is renowned for its matcha (green tea) sweets. Indulge in matcha-flavored treats like matcha-flavored mochi, matcha parfaits, and matcha-flavored wagashi (traditional Japanese sweets).

Recommended Places: Tsujiri, Gion Tsujiri, Nakamura Tokichi Honten

6. Kyo Kaiseki Sushi:

Description: Experience the unique combination of kaiseki and sushi in Kyoto. Fresh, seasonal ingredients are artfully arranged to create a fusion of traditional kaiseki and sushi flavors.

Recommended Places: Ganko Sushi, Izuu, Musashi Sushi

7. Kyoto Soba (Buckwheat Noodles):

Description: Try Kyoto-style soba, featuring thin buckwheat noodles served hot or cold. Pair them with

dipping sauces or enjoy them in a hot broth with seasonal toppings.
Recommended Places: Honke Owariya, Omen, Izuu

8. Kyo Wagashi (Traditional Sweets):
Description: Kyoto's wagashi are traditional sweets often enjoyed with tea. Delicate and artistic, these sweets reflect the seasons and are crafted with precision.
Recommended Places: Yatsuhashi Tsujiri, Ganko Sushi, Toraya Kyoto Ichijo

9. Kyoto Kappo Cuisine:
Description: Kappo cuisine involves skillfully prepared dishes in an intimate setting. Enjoy the chef's creations, which often include fresh seafood, seasonal vegetables, and intricate presentations.
Recommended Places: Ganko Sushi, Arashiyama Kikusui, Ryozanpaku

10. Nishiki Market Street Food:
Description: Navigate Nishiki Market for a street food adventure. Sample a variety of local bites, from grilled skewers to pickled vegetables and Kyoto-style sushi.
Recommended Places: Various stalls within Nishiki Market

11. Kyo Kaiseki Vegetarian:
Description: Explore vegetarian kaiseki options that showcase Kyoto's dedication to seasonal, plant-based cuisine. These meals offer a unique culinary experience without meat or fish.

Recommended Places: Ajiroan, Tosuiro, Ganko Sushi

12. Sakura Mochi:
Description: During cherry blossom season, indulge in sakura mochi, a sweet rice cake filled with red bean paste and wrapped in a pickled cherry blossom leaf. It's a seasonal delicacy.
Recommended Places: Various wagashi shops

Kyoto's culinary scene not only satisfies the palate but also reflects the city's cultural heritage. Whether you're savoring the intricacies of kaiseki or enjoying a casual stroll through Nishiki Market, each culinary experience in Kyoto is a flavorful journey through tradition and innovation.

Chapter 6: Experiencing Osaka

Osaka, often referred to as the "Kitchen of Japan," is a vibrant city known for its delicious street food, historic landmarks, and lively atmosphere. Dive into the heart of Osaka's unique charm with these experiences:

1. Osaka Street Food Extravaganza:
   Description: Explore Dotonbori and Kuromon Ichiba Market for a street food adventure. Sample Osaka's iconic takoyaki (octopus balls), okonomiyaki (savory pancakes), and kushikatsu (deep-fried skewers).
   Must-Try Spots: Mizuno Okonomiyaki, Kuromon Ichiba Market stalls, Kushikatsu Daruma

2. Osaka Castle and Nishinomaru Garden:
   Description: Immerse yourself in history at Osaka Castle. Explore the majestic castle grounds and enjoy a stroll through Nishinomaru Garden, especially during cherry blossom season for breathtaking views.
   Recommended Visit Time: Half a day

3. Kuromon Ichiba Market:
   Description: Delight in Kuromon Ichiba Market's bustling atmosphere. Discover fresh seafood, fruits, and local snacks. Engage with vendors and indulge in Osaka's culinary delights.

Must-Try Foods: Takoyaki, okonomiyaki, fresh seafood, Kobe beef skewers

4. Shinsaibashi Shopping Arcade:
Description: Dive into the vibrant energy of Shinsaibashi, a bustling shopping arcade. Explore a mix of traditional and trendy shops, boutiques, and eateries.
Recommended for: Shopping, dining, and street fashion

5. Dotonbori District:
Description: Experience the iconic Dotonbori district, known for its neon lights and lively entertainment. Stroll along the canal, admire the Glico Running Man sign, and explore the vibrant streets.
Must-See: Glico Running Man sign, Ebisu Bridge, entertainment theaters

6. Osaka Aquarium Kaiyukan:
Description: Dive into the wonders of the ocean at Osaka Aquarium Kaiyukan. Encounter marine life from different regions and experience the awe-inspiring central tank.
Recommended Visit Time: Half a day

7. Sumiyoshi Taisha Shrine:
Description: Visit Sumiyoshi Taisha, one of Japan's oldest Shinto shrines. Cross its distinctive arched bridge and appreciate the architectural beauty of this historic site.
Recommended for: Cultural and spiritual exploration

8. Umeda Sky Building:
Description: Enjoy panoramic views of Osaka from the Umeda Sky Building. Take the escalator ride through the Floating Garden Observatory for a unique perspective of the city.
Recommended Visit Time: Evening for sunset views

9. Osaka Ramen Tasting:
Description: Osaka is a ramen lover's paradise. Try different styles of ramen, from the rich and savory tonkotsu to the soy-based shoyu ramen, at local ramen shops.
Must-Try Spots: Ippudo, Ikkousha, Menya Hanabi

10. Tempozan Ferris Wheel:
Description: Experience Osaka's skyline from the Tempozan Ferris Wheel. Especially enchanting in the evening, it offers stunning views of Osaka Bay and the city lights.
Recommended Visit Time: Evening for city lights

11. Osaka Museum of History:
Description: Gain insights into Osaka's past at the Osaka Museum of History. The observatory deck provides panoramic views of the city skyline.
Recommended Visit Time: Half a day

12. Namba Yasaka Shrine and Hozenji Yokocho Alley:
Description: Explore the tranquil Namba Yasaka Shrine and the nearby Hozenji Yokocho Alley. Witness

the contrast between the serene shrine and the lively atmosphere of the historic alley.
Recommended for: Cultural exploration and dining

Osaka's dynamic blend of culinary delights, historical landmarks, and modern attractions creates a tapestry of experiences. Whether you're savoring street food in Dotonbori or exploring the cultural gems of Sumiyoshi Taisha, Osaka promises a captivating journey through its rich heritage and contemporary allure.

Modern Entertainment in Osaka

Osaka, a city known for its rich history, also pulsates with modern entertainment options. From cutting-edge technology to vibrant nightlife, experience the contemporary side of Osaka with these dynamic attractions:

1. Universal Studios Japan:
    Description: Step into the magical world of Universal Studios Japan (USJ). Enjoy thrilling rides, immersive attractions based on blockbuster movies, and live entertainment shows.
    Must-Experience: The Wizarding World of Harry Potter, Hollywood Dream The Ride, and Minion Park.

2. Osaka Aquarium Kaiyukan After Dark:
Description: Experience the enchanting Osaka Aquarium Kaiyukan in the evening. The After Dark program allows visitors to explore the aquarium after regular hours, creating a magical atmosphere.
Recommended Visit Time: Evening

3. Namba Parks Shopping and Entertainment Complex:
Description: Indulge in shopping, dining, and entertainment at Namba Parks. The complex features a unique terraced garden, a range of stores, and diverse dining options.
Must-Visit: The rooftop garden with its scenic views.

4. Osaka Castle Illuminage:
Description: Witness the spectacular illumination of Osaka Castle during the Osaka Castle Illuminage event. The castle grounds are adorned with enchanting lights, creating a magical ambiance.
Recommended Visit Time: Evening during the illuminations.

5. Dotonbori River Cruise:
Description: Glide along the Dotonbori canal on a river cruise. Experience the vibrant energy of Dotonbori's neon lights, iconic signs, and lively entertainment districts from the water.
Recommended Visit Time: Evening for illuminated views.

6. Tsutenkaku Tower and Shinsekai District:
Description: Explore the retro-futuristic atmosphere of the Shinsekai district around Tsutenkaku Tower. Enjoy a variety of entertainment options, including shops, restaurants, and street performances.

Must-Visit: Billiken, the god of things as they ought to be, located near Tsutenkaku Tower.

7. Osaka Science Museum:
Description: Engage in hands-on exhibits and interactive displays at the Osaka Science Museum. Explore the wonders of science and technology in an engaging and educational setting.

Recommended Visit Time: Half a day

8. Tempozan Ferris Wheel and Kaiyukan Aqua Gate:
Description: Combine modern entertainment with scenic views. Enjoy a ride on the Tempozan Ferris Wheel and visit the Kaiyukan Aqua Gate, an interactive digital art installation.

Recommended Visit Time: Evening for Ferris Wheel views.

9. Hep Five Ferris Wheel:
Description: Take a spin on the iconic Hep Five Ferris Wheel located in the Umeda district. Enjoy panoramic views of the cityscape from this vibrant entertainment complex.

Recommended Visit Time: Evening for city lights.

10. Umeda Sky Building Floating Garden Observatory:
Description: Soar to the top of the Umeda Sky Building for panoramic views. The Floating Garden Observatory offers a unique vantage point to appreciate Osaka's skyline.
Recommended Visit Time: Evening for sunset views.

11. Nightlife in Namba and Umeda:
Description: Experience Osaka's lively nightlife in districts like Namba and Umeda. Explore bars, clubs, and entertainment hubs for a taste of the city's after-dark energy.
Recommended for: Night owls and those seeking vibrant nightlife.

12. Live Music at Zepp Namba:
Description: Catch a live music performance at Zepp Namba, a popular concert venue. Check the schedule for upcoming shows spanning various genres.
Must-Experience: A live performance by a favorite artist or band.

Osaka's modern entertainment offerings complement its historical charm, creating a dynamic cityscape that caters to diverse tastes. Whether you're exploring theme parks, enjoying illuminated landmarks, or embracing the lively nightlife, Osaka's contemporary allure promises an unforgettable experience.

Osaka's Street Food Paradise

Osaka's street food scene is a vibrant and flavorful journey, offering a delightful array of local specialties. Dive into the heart of this culinary paradise with these must-try street foods:

1. Takoyaki:
   Description: Osaka's iconic street food, takoyaki, are savory octopus balls. Watch as skilled vendors pour batter into spherical molds, add a piece of octopus, and skillfully flip the balls until golden brown.
   Must-Try Spots: Takoyaki Doraku Wanaka, Gindaco, and Takoya Dotonbori Kukuru

2. Okonomiyaki:
   Description: Okonomiyaki is a savory pancake filled with ingredients like cabbage, pork, and seafood. Cooked on a griddle, it's often topped with a special okonomiyaki sauce, mayo, and bonito flakes.
   Must-Try Spots: Chibo Okonomiyaki, Mizuno Okonomiyaki, and Hiroshima Okonomiyaki Chitose

3. Kushikatsu:
   Description: Deep-fried skewers, or kushikatsu, feature a variety of ingredients like meat, vegetables, and seafood. Dip them in a communal sauce, but remember, double-dipping is a no-no!
   Must-Try Spots: Kushikatsu Daruma, Yaekatsu, and Kushikatsu Bar Zin

4. Takosen:
Description: Takoyaki meets senbei (rice cracker) in takosen. A crispy senbei is topped with a mini takoyaki, creating a delightful fusion of textures and flavors.

Must-Try Spots: Takoyaki Doraku Wanaka, Takosenya Namba, and Takosen Monja Shirokuma

5. Negiyaki:
Description: Negiyaki is a savory pancake filled with green onions and other ingredients. Often compared to okonomiyaki, negiyaki is lighter and emphasizes the flavors of the green onions.

Must-Try Spots: Negiyaki Yamamoto, Ajinoya, and Negiyaki Issen Yoshoku

6. Ikayaki:
Description: Grilled or fried squid on a stick, known as ikayaki, is a popular street food. The squid is often basted with a savory soy-based sauce, creating a delicious and portable snack.

Must-Try Spots: Ikayaki Chidoya, Ikayaki Oomasa, and Ikayaki Okiyama

7. Korokke:
Description: Korokke are Japanese croquettes, typically made with mashed potatoes or ground meat coated in breadcrumbs and deep-fried. Varieties include beef, shrimp, and vegetable korokke.

Must-Try Spots: Croquette Shop Korokke Hirota, Korokke Taro, and Korokke Shinkaraku

8. Yakitori:
Description: Skewered and grilled chicken, or yakitori, is a popular street food in Osaka. Enjoy various parts of the chicken, including thighs, wings, and skin, seasoned and cooked to perfection.

Must-Try Spots: Kushikatsu Daruma, Yakitori Ichiraku, and Torikizoku

9. Obanyaki:
Description: Obanyaki are sweet filled pastries resembling small pancakes. Common fillings include sweet red bean paste, custard, chocolate, and seasonal fruits.

Must-Try Spots: Obanyaki Abeno, Obanyaki Fujiya, and Obanyaki Maito

10. Katsu Sando:
Description: Katsu Sando is a Japanese sandwich featuring a breaded and deep-fried cutlet, usually pork or beef, sandwiched between soft white bread with tonkatsu sauce and mustard.

Must-Try Spots: Maisen, Tonkatsu Yachiyo, and Katsukura

11. Dango:
Description: Dango are skewered rice dumplings served with various toppings. Common variations include mitarashi (sweet soy glaze), anko (sweet red bean paste), and kinako (roasted soybean flour).

Must-Try Spots: Dango Juhachiro, Kamo Dango, and Hanami Dango

12. Taiyaki:

Description: Taiyaki are fish-shaped pastries filled with sweet fillings like red bean paste, custard, or chocolate. Crispy on the outside and soft on the inside, they're a delightful street treat.

Must-Try Spots: Taiyaki Wakaba, Taiyaki Kaneko Hannosuke, and Taiyaki Dotonbori Tachibana

Osaka's street food paradise invites you to embark on a culinary adventure, savoring these delectable treats while immersing yourself in the city's lively atmosphere. Whether you're exploring Dotonbori or Kuromon Ichiba Market, each bite offers a taste of Osaka's culinary creativity and cultural richness.

Osaka's Shopping Extravaganza

Osaka, a city renowned for its vibrant atmosphere, offers a diverse shopping experience that caters to every taste. From bustling markets to luxury boutiques, here's your guide to Osaka's shopping extravaganza:

1. Shinsaibashi Shopping Street:
   Description: Explore the bustling Shinsaibashi Shopping Street, a bustling arcade filled with a mix of international brands, local boutiques, and unique shops. It's a shopping haven for fashion enthusiasts.
   Must-Visit: Daimaru Shinsaibashi, Shinsaibashi-suji Shopping Arcade, and American Village.

2. Namba Parks:
   Description: Namba Parks is a modern shopping complex that combines retail therapy with green spaces. Discover a variety of shops, restaurants, and entertainment options within its unique terraced structure.
   Must-Visit: Rooftop garden, specialty stores, and the Cinema Complex.

3. Dotonbori:
   Description: Dive into the lively atmosphere of Dotonbori, a district known for its vibrant signage, entertainment, and shopping. Explore the riverside area for unique boutiques and iconic landmarks.
   Must-Visit: Glico Running Man sign, Namba Ebisu Shrine, and Dotonbori Canal.

4. Kuromon Ichiba Market:
   Description: While renowned for its fresh produce and street food, Kuromon Ichiba Market is also a shopping destination. Discover stalls offering local delicacies, snacks, and unique kitchenware.

Must-Visit: Fresh seafood stalls, street food vendors, and specialty shops.

5. Hankyu Umeda Main Store:
Description: Immerse yourself in luxury shopping at Hankyu Umeda Main Store. This department store showcases high-end fashion, cosmetics, and lifestyle brands.

Must-Visit: Luxury boutiques, international brands, and the food floor.

6. Grand Front Osaka:
Description: Grand Front Osaka is a modern complex housing an array of shops, dining options, and entertainment. Discover both Japanese and international brands in this sleek shopping destination.

Must-Visit: Knowledge Capital, Umekita Plaza, and the variety of shops.

7. Tenjinbashisuji Shopping Street:
Description: Stroll along Tenjinbashisuji Shopping Street, one of the longest shopping streets in Japan. Find a mix of traditional and modern shops, offering clothing, accessories, and local goods.

Must-Visit: Traditional storefronts, local boutiques, and the vibrant street atmosphere.

8. Hep Five:
Description: Hep Five is a distinctive shopping and entertainment complex in Umeda. Recognized by its

iconic red Ferris wheel, it houses a variety of shops, restaurants, and entertainment venues.

Must-Visit: Ferris wheel for panoramic views, fashion boutiques, and unique shops.

9. Osaka Station City:

Description: Osaka Station City is a major transportation hub with an extensive shopping area. Discover a mix of department stores, fashion brands, and specialty shops within the station complex.

Must-Visit: Grand Front Osaka, Lucua Osaka, and the underground shopping area.

10. Abeno Harukas:

Description: Abeno Harukas is not only Japan's tallest building but also a shopping and entertainment complex. Enjoy shopping in a modern setting with stunning views of the city.

Must-Visit: Kintetsu Department Store, Abeno Harukas Art Museum, and the observation deck.

11. Minami (Namba) District:

Description: Dive into the trendy Minami (Namba) district for fashionable boutiques, electronics stores, and quirky shops. The area offers a mix of contemporary and traditional shopping experiences.

Must-Visit: Namba Parks, Namba Walk, and the bustling Namba area.

12. Senba Center Building:
Description: Senba Center Building is a hidden gem for those seeking unique fashion finds. Explore the various boutiques and shops offering a range of clothing, accessories, and lifestyle items.

Must-Visit: Independent boutiques, vintage shops, and eclectic fashion stores.

Osaka's shopping extravaganza caters to diverse tastes, from luxury seekers to those in search of unique local finds. Whether you're strolling through Shinsaibashi or exploring the markets in Kuromon Ichiba, each shopping district adds a layer to Osaka's dynamic retail landscape.

Chapter 7: Day Trips and Excursions

Osaka's strategic location makes it an excellent hub for day trips and excursions to nearby attractions. Experience the beauty of the Kansai region with these captivating day trips:

1. Kyoto:
Travel Time: Approximately 15-30 minutes by train.
    Highlights: Explore Kyoto's historic temples, traditional tea houses, and serene gardens. Visit iconic landmarks like Fushimi Inari Shrine, Kinkaku-ji (Golden Pavilion), and Kiyomizu-dera.

2. Nara:
Travel Time: Approximately 30-45 minutes by train.
    Highlights: Encounter friendly deer at Nara Park, home to Todai-ji Temple and the Great Buddha. Explore Kasuga Taisha Shrine and stroll through the charming streets of Naramachi.

3. Kobe:
Travel Time: Approximately 20-30 minutes by train.
    Highlights: Discover the cosmopolitan city of Kobe. Visit the historic Kitano district, explore Meriken Park, and savor world-renowned Kobe beef in the bustling Motomachi area.

4. Himeji:
Travel Time: Approximately 30-60 minutes by train.
Highlights: Marvel at Himeji Castle, a UNESCO World Heritage site known for its stunning white facade. Explore the castle grounds, Kokoen Garden, and the nearby Engyo-ji Temple.

5. Osaka Bay Area:
Travel Time: Varies (accessible by train or boat).
Highlights: Enjoy family-friendly attractions at Universal Studios Japan, visit Osaka Aquarium Kaiyukan, and explore the modern entertainment complex of Tempozan Harbor Village.

6. Wakayama:
Travel Time: Approximately 1-2 hours by train.
Highlights: Experience the spiritual atmosphere at Mount Koya (Koyasan), a sacred mountain with numerous temples. Explore the lush Kumano Kodo pilgrimage trails and visit Wakayama Castle.

7. Amanohashidate:
Travel Time: Approximately 2-3 hours by train.
Highlights: Take in the scenic beauty of Amanohashidate, known as the "Bridge to Heaven." Enjoy a stroll across the sandbar, visit the Amanohashidate View Land observation deck, and explore nearby temples.

8. Kinosaki Onsen:
Travel Time: Approximately 2 hours by train.

Highlights: Immerse yourself in the tranquil atmosphere of Kinosaki Onsen. Enjoy a picturesque stroll along the willow-lined canals, visit seven public bathhouses, and experience the town's traditional charm.

9. Ise-Shima:
Travel Time: Approximately 2-3 hours by train.

Highlights: Visit Ise Grand Shrine, one of Japan's most important Shinto shrines. Explore the scenic coastline of the Shima Peninsula, and discover pearl cultivation at Mikimoto Pearl Island.

10. Yoshino:
Travel Time: Approximately 1-2 hours by train.

Highlights: Witness the beauty of cherry blossoms in Yoshino, particularly during sakura season. Explore Mount Yoshino's enchanting slopes adorned with thousands of cherry trees.

11. Hikone:
Travel Time: Approximately 1-2 hours by train.

Highlights: Visit Hikone Castle, one of Japan's original and well-preserved castles. Explore Genkyuen Garden and take a boat cruise on Lake Biwa for picturesque views.

12. Katsuo-ji Temple:
Travel Time: Approximately 1 hour by train.
Highlights: Discover the unique Katsuo-ji Temple known for its "daruma" dolls. Experience the serene atmosphere, stroll through the temple grounds, and participate in daruma-related activities.

These day trips and excursions from Osaka offer a diverse range of experiences, from cultural immersion to natural beauty. Whether you're exploring ancient temples in Kyoto, enjoying onsen relaxation in Kinosaki, or savoring Kobe's culinary delights, each destination adds a layer to your Kansai adventure.

Nearby Destinations From Tokyo

While Tokyo itself is a vast and dynamic metropolis, there are several nearby destinations that offer unique experiences and cultural richness. Venture beyond the city limits with these captivating day trips:

1. Yokohama:
Travel Time: Approximately 30 minutes by train.
Highlights: Explore Yokohama's waterfront attractions, including Minato Mirai 21, Landmark Tower, and the historic Sankeien Garden. Don't miss the CupNoodles Museum and Yokohama Chinatown.

2. Kamakura:
Travel Time: Approximately 1 hour by train.
Highlights: Discover Kamakura's iconic Great Buddha at Kotoku-in, explore the serene Hokoku-ji Bamboo Forest, and visit Tsurugaoka Hachimangu Shrine. Enjoy the coastal atmosphere and hiking trails.

3. Nikko:
Travel Time: Approximately 2 hours by train.
Highlights: Visit the UNESCO World Heritage site of Toshogu Shrine, explore the natural beauty of Nikko National Park, and take in the stunning Kegon Falls. Don't miss the sacred Lake Chuzenji.

4. Hakone:
Travel Time: Approximately 2 hours by train.
Highlights: Experience hot springs, cruise on Lake Ashi with views of Mt. Fuji, and explore the Hakone Open-Air Museum. Hakone is renowned for its scenic landscapes and relaxing onsen resorts.

5. Kawagoe (Little Edo):
Travel Time: Approximately 30 minutes by train.
Highlights: Step back in time as you explore the well-preserved Edo-period architecture of Kawagoe. Visit Kurazukuri Street, try local snacks like sweet potato ice cream, and stroll through Kashiya Yokocho.

6. Chichibu:
Travel Time: Approximately 1.5 hours by train.
Highlights: Discover the natural beauty of Chichibu, including the scenic Arakawa River and Mitsumine Shrine. Visit Hitsujiyama Park during spring for vibrant flower fields.

7. Mount Takao:
Travel Time: Approximately 1 hour by train.
Highlights: Enjoy nature and outdoor activities at Mount Takao. Hike to the summit for panoramic views, visit the Yakuoin Temple, and savor local cuisine at the mountain's restaurants.

8. Enoshima and Kamakura:
Travel Time: Approximately 1 hour by train.
Highlights: Combine visits to Enoshima Island, known for its shrines and sea views, with Kamakura's cultural attractions. Explore the Enoshima Aquarium, Hase-dera Temple, and the vibrant Enoshima street scene.

9. Odaiba:
Travel Time: Approximately 30 minutes by train.
Highlights: Experience entertainment and shopping in Odaiba. Visit attractions like Palette Town, teamLab Borderless digital art museum, and enjoy the waterfront at Odaiba Seaside Park.

10. Kawasaki:
Travel Time: Approximately 20 minutes by train.

Highlights: Explore Kawasaki's unique attractions, including Kawasaki Daishi Temple, Kawasaki Warehouse (a retro gaming arcade), and the annual Kawasaki Halloween Parade.

11. Izu Peninsula:
Travel Time: Approximately 2-3 hours by train.

Highlights: Discover the scenic Izu Peninsula with hot springs, coastal views, and beautiful beaches. Explore places like Jogasaki Coast, Shuzenji Onsen, and the historic town of Shimoda.

12. Tama Zoological Park:
Travel Time: Approximately 30 minutes by train.

Highlights: Enjoy a day at Tama Zoological Park, home to a wide variety of animals. Explore the expansive grounds, attend animal shows, and engage in educational exhibits.

These nearby destinations from Tokyo provide a diverse range of experiences, from historical exploration to natural beauty. Whether you're escaping to the hot springs of Hakone or immersing yourself in the charm of Kamakura, each destination offers a unique facet of Japan's rich cultural tapestry.

Nearby Destinations From Kyoto

Kyoto, steeped in history and tradition, is surrounded by enchanting destinations that offer a glimpse into Japan's cultural richness. Embark on these captivating day trips from Kyoto:

1. Nara:
Travel Time: Approximately 45 minutes by train.
    Highlights: Encounter friendly deer at Nara Park, explore Todai-ji Temple housing the Great Buddha, and visit Kasuga Taisha Shrine with its lantern-lined paths.

2. Osaka:
Travel Time: Approximately 15-30 minutes by train.
    Highlights: Discover Osaka's vibrant street food in Dotonbori, explore Osaka Castle, and experience modern entertainment at Universal Studios Japan.

3. Uji:
Travel Time: Approximately 20 minutes by train.
    Highlights: Explore the historic Byodoin Temple, stroll along the scenic Uji River, and indulge in Uji's famous matcha (green tea) sweets and drinks.

今　佛は常にいませども
現ならぬぞ　あはれなる
人の音せぬ　暁に
ほのかに夢に　見え給ふ

4. Arashiyama and Sagano:
Travel Time: Approximately 30 minutes by train.
Highlights: Visit the iconic Arashiyama Bamboo Grove, explore the Iwatayama Monkey Park, and experience a serene boat ride along the Hozugawa River.

5. Kibune and Kurama:
Travel Time: Approximately 30 minutes by train.
Highlights: Hike through the lush mountains connecting Kibune and Kurama, visit the Kurama-dera Temple, and enjoy a traditional kaiseki meal at a riverside restaurant in Kibune.

6. Ohara:
Travel Time: Approximately 1 hour by bus.
Highlights: Explore the rural charm of Ohara, visit Sanzen-in Temple surrounded by beautiful gardens, and discover Ohara's unique agricultural landscapes.

7. Hikone:
Travel Time: Approximately 1 hour by train.
Highlights: Explore Hikone Castle, one of Japan's original castles, stroll through Genkyuen Garden, and enjoy panoramic views of Lake Biwa.

8. Kinosaki Onsen:
Travel Time: Approximately 2 hours by train.
Highlights: Immerse yourself in the tranquil atmosphere of Kinosaki Onsen. Experience the town's seven public bathhouses and picturesque willow-lined canals.

9. Amanohashidate:
Travel Time: Approximately 2-3 hours by train.
Highlights: Admire the scenic "Bridge to Heaven" at Amanohashidate, take a cable car to Amanohashidate View Land, and explore the enchanting sandbar.

10. Biwako Valley:
Travel Time: Approximately 1-1.5 hours by train.
Highlights: Enjoy outdoor activities at Biwako Valley, including hiking, zip-lining, and seasonal attractions like snow sports in winter and lush greenery in summer.

11. Kameoka and Hozugawa River Boat Ride:
Travel Time: Approximately 30 minutes by train.
Highlights: Take a scenic boat ride along the Hozugawa River, passing through picturesque landscapes, and explore the rural beauty of Kameoka.

12. Ise-Shima:
Travel Time: Approximately 2-3 hours by train.
Highlights: Visit Ise Grand Shrine, explore the scenic coastline of the Shima Peninsula, and discover pearl cultivation at Mikimoto Pearl Island.

These nearby destinations from Kyoto offer a diverse range of experiences, from spiritual encounters in Nara to the tranquil onsen retreats in Kinosaki. Each destination unveils a unique aspect of Japan's cultural heritage and natural beauty, complementing Kyoto's historical charm.

Nearby Destinations in Osaka

Osaka's central location in the Kansai region opens the door to a myriad of captivating nearby destinations. Venture beyond Osaka's vibrant cityscape and discover these enchanting day trips:

1. Kyoto:
Travel Time: Approximately 15-30 minutes by train.
   Highlights: Immerse yourself in Kyoto's historical charm with visits to iconic landmarks like Fushimi Inari Shrine, Kinkaku-ji (Golden Pavilion), and the historic Gion district.

2. Nara:
Travel Time: Approximately 30-45 minutes by train.
   Highlights: Encounter friendly deer at Nara Park, explore Todai-ji Temple and the Great Buddha, and wander through the picturesque Naramachi district.

3. Kobe:
Travel Time: Approximately 20-30 minutes by train.
   Highlights: Indulge in Kobe's culinary delights, explore the historic Kitano district, and enjoy the scenic views from the Shin-Kobe Ropeway.

4. Himeji:
Travel Time: Approximately 30-60 minutes by train.
   Highlights: Marvel at Himeji Castle, a UNESCO World Heritage site. Explore the castle grounds, Kokoen Garden, and nearby attractions like Engyo-ji Temple.

Kyoto

5. Osaka Bay Area:
Travel Time: Varies (accessible by train or boat).
Highlights: Experience family-friendly attractions at Universal Studios Japan, explore Osaka Aquarium Kaiyukan, and enjoy the entertainment complex of Tempozan Harbor Village.

6. Wakayama:
Travel Time: Approximately 1-2 hours by train.
Highlights: Experience the spiritual atmosphere at Mount Koya (Koyasan), explore Kumano Kodo pilgrimage trails, and visit Wakayama Castle.

7. Amanohashidate:
Travel Time: Approximately 2-3 hours by train.
Highlights: Admire the scenic "Bridge to Heaven" at Amanohashidate, explore the sandbar, and visit the Amanohashidate View Land observation deck.

8. Kinosaki Onsen:
Travel Time: Approximately 2 hours by train.
Highlights: Relax in the tranquil atmosphere of Kinosaki Onsen, featuring seven public bathhouses, picturesque canals, and a charming townscape.

9. Ise-Shima:
Travel Time: Approximately 2-3 hours by train.
Highlights: Visit Ise Grand Shrine, explore the scenic coastline of the Shima Peninsula, and discover pearl cultivation at Mikimoto Pearl Island.

10. Biwako Valley:
Travel Time: Approximately 1-1.5 hours by train.
Highlights: Enjoy outdoor activities at Biwako Valley, including hiking, zip-lining, and seasonal attractions like snow sports in winter.

11. Kameoka and Hozugawa River Boat Ride:
Travel Time: Approximately 30 minutes by train.
Highlights: Experience a scenic boat ride along the Hozugawa River, passing through picturesque landscapes, and explore the rural beauty of Kameoka.

12. Tottori Sand Dunes:
Travel Time: Approximately 2-3 hours by train.
Highlights: Discover the unique landscape of Tottori Sand Dunes, explore Sand Museum showcasing intricate sand sculptures, and enjoy coastal views.

These nearby destinations from Osaka offer a diverse range of experiences, from cultural exploration in Kyoto to seaside retreats in Wakayama. Whether you're seeking historical landmarks, natural beauty, or culinary delights, each destination provides a unique addition to your Kansai journey.

Nature Escapes in Tokyo

While Tokyo is renowned for its bustling urban life, the city also boasts serene natural escapes that offer a refreshing break. Discover these tranquil havens within and around Tokyo:

1. Shinjuku Gyoen National Garden:
Description: A harmonious blend of Japanese, English, and French garden landscapes. Enjoy the cherry blossoms in spring, serene ponds, and wide-open lawns.
Highlights: Traditional tea houses, greenhouse with tropical plants, and seasonal flower displays.

2. Ueno Park:
Description: A vast public park with tree-lined paths, open spaces, and cultural attractions. Ideal for leisurely walks, picnics, and enjoying the scenic Shinobazu Pond.
Highlights: Ueno Zoo, museums including Tokyo National Museum, and cherry blossoms in spring.

3. Inokashira Park:
Description: A peaceful park surrounding Inokashira Pond. Rent a rowboat, stroll along tree-lined paths, and experience the serene atmosphere.
Highlights: Ghibli Museum, cherry blossoms in spring, and a variety of street performers.

4. Mount Takao:

Description: A popular hiking destination with multiple trails for varying levels of difficulty. Reach the summit for panoramic views of Tokyo and beyond.

Highlights: Yakuoin Temple, cable car or chairlift options, and seasonal festivals.

5. Showa Kinen Park:

Description: A spacious park with expansive lawns, cycling paths, and themed gardens. Perfect for outdoor activities, picnics, and enjoying the changing seasons.

Highlights: Japanese garden, cherry blossoms in spring, and colorful autumn foliage.

6. Odaiba Seaside Park:

Description: A waterfront park offering stunning views of Tokyo Bay and the Rainbow Bridge. Relax on the sandy beach, stroll along the promenade, and enjoy recreational activities.

Highlights: Palette Town, Odaiba Marine Park, and occasional events.

7. Hamarikyu Gardens:

Description: A traditional Japanese garden with tidal ponds and meticulously landscaped greenery. Experience the tranquility amidst skyscrapers in the nearby Shiodome district.

Highlights: Tea house, cherry blossoms in spring, and seasonal flower displays.

8. Todoroki Valley:
Description: A hidden gem offering a nature walk along a wooded ravine. Cross wooden bridges, explore the lush greenery, and discover the Todoroki Fudo Temple.
Highlights: Todoroki Fudo Temple, natural hot spring foot bath, and a serene atmosphere.

9. Mitaka City Nature Observation Park:
Description: A peaceful park with walking trails, ponds, and natural landscapes. Ideal for birdwatching, nature observation, and a quiet retreat.
Highlights: Birdwatching spots, seasonal flowers, and peaceful surroundings.

10. Okutama:
Description: Venture to the outskirts of Tokyo for a nature retreat in Okutama. Enjoy hiking trails, pristine rivers, and lush forests away from the urban hustle.
Highlights: Okutama Lake, Mitake Valley, and hiking routes like the Okutama Mukashi Michi Trail.

11. Tama Zoological Park:
Description: A zoological park with a focus on spacious and naturalistic enclosures. Experience a blend of wildlife observation and outdoor surroundings.
Highlights: Asiatic lions, Edo Market Zone, and seasonal events.

12. Rikugien Gardens:
   Description: A classic Japanese garden featuring a central pond, walking paths, and meticulously designed landscapes. Enjoy the serene ambiance in every season.
   Highlights: Illumination events, traditional tea house, and cherry blossoms in spring.

These nature escapes in Tokyo provide a peaceful respite from the city's hustle and bustle, allowing you to connect with nature and experience moments of tranquility within the metropolis.

Nature Escapes in Kyoto

Nature Escapes in Kyoto: Serenity Amidst Timeless Beauty

Kyoto, a city steeped in tradition, also offers serene natural escapes that transport you to a world of tranquility. Immerse yourself in the beauty of nature with these captivating spots in and around Kyoto:

1. Arashiyama Bamboo Grove:
   Description: Walk through enchanting bamboo groves, creating a serene and otherworldly atmosphere. The Sagano Bamboo Forest is particularly magical during early mornings.
   Highlights: Iwatayama Monkey Park, Togetsukyo Bridge, and Tenryu-ji Temple.

2. Kibune and Kurama:
Description: Venture into the mountains to explore Kibune and Kurama. Hike through lush landscapes, visit temples, and experience the serene connection with nature.
Highlights: Kibune Shrine, Kurama-dera Temple, and the Kifune Shrine.

3. Philosopher's Path:
Description: A scenic canal-side path lined with hundreds of cherry trees. Stroll along the Philosopher's Path, especially during cherry blossom season, for a contemplative experience.
Highlights: Eikando Temple, Nanzen-ji Temple, and the picturesque canal.

4. Ohara:
Description: A rural retreat surrounded by mountains and lush landscapes. Discover the tranquility of Ohara with its unique temples, gardens, and traditional agricultural scenery.
Highlights: Sanzen-in Temple, Jakkoin Temple, and the Ohara Museum of Art.

5. Tadasu no Mori Forest:
Description: Located around the Shimogamo Shrine, this sacred forest provides a peaceful retreat within the city. Enjoy serene walks among the towering trees.
Highlights: Shimogamo Shrine, Mitarai Pond, and the atmospheric forest trails.

6. Mount Hiei:
Description: A sacred mountain with hiking trails and panoramic views of Kyoto. Accessible by cable car or a challenging hike, Mount Hiei offers a serene escape.
Highlights: Enryaku-ji Temple, Biwako Valley, and the beautiful scenery.

7. Kameoka and Hozugawa River:
Description: Experience a tranquil boat ride along the Hozugawa River, surrounded by scenic landscapes. Explore the rural beauty of Kameoka and enjoy the river's gentle flow.
Highlights: Hozugawa River Boat Ride, Kameoka Castle, and the natural beauty along the riverbanks.

8. Ohnanami Pond at Daigo-ji Temple:
Description: Discover the serene beauty of Ohnanami Pond within the expansive Daigo-ji Temple complex. The reflection of cherry blossoms on the pond is particularly stunning.
Highlights: Daigo-ji Temple's Five-story Pagoda, Benten Hall, and the historic gardens.

9. Rurikoin Temple:
Description: A hidden gem nestled in the mountains, Rurikoin Temple offers a stunning moss garden and seasonal views. Visit during autumn for vibrant foliage.
Highlights: Moss garden, seasonal flower displays, and the peaceful ambiance.

10. Kifune Shrine:
Description: Located in a forested area near Kurama, Kifune Shrine offers a peaceful retreat. Explore the shrine's serene surroundings and enjoy the atmospheric setting.
Highlights: Kibune Shrine, traditional Japanese tea houses, and the mystical ambiance.

11. Hozugawa Kudari (Boat Ride):
Description: Drift along the Hozugawa River on a traditional boat ride, surrounded by lush landscapes. Experience the gentle currents and scenic beauty.
Highlights: Riverside scenery, traditional boat ride experience, and the natural beauty along the riverbanks.

12. Kyoto Botanical Garden:
Description: Explore diverse plant collections and themed gardens in this peaceful botanical haven. A perfect spot for a leisurely stroll and nature appreciation.
Highlights: Sakura Alleé, Bamboo Grove, and the greenhouse with tropical plants.

These nature escapes in Kyoto offer a harmonious blend of natural beauty and cultural richness, providing a serene contrast to the city's historic landmarks and bustling streets.

Nature Escapes in Osaka

While Osaka is known for its vibrant city life, there are serene natural escapes that offer a peaceful respite. Immerse yourself in nature with these captivating spots in and around Osaka:

1. Minoo Park:
   Description: A picturesque park famous for its hiking trails, Minoo Park is particularly enchanting during the autumn foliage season. The park is home to a stunning waterfall and charming walking paths.
   Highlights: Minoo Waterfall, walking trails, and seasonal cherry blossoms and autumn foliage.

2. Katsuo-ji Temple:
   Description: Nestled in the mountains, Katsuo-ji Temple is known for its serene surroundings and numerous "daruma" dolls. Enjoy a peaceful escape with beautiful gardens and temple structures.
   Highlights: Daruma dolls, scenic temple grounds, and tranquil mountain setting.

3. Mount Koya (Koyasan):
   Description: A sacred mountain retreat, Mount Koya offers a serene escape with atmospheric temples and stunning landscapes. Explore the peaceful cemetery, Okunoin, and experience Buddhist culture.
   Highlights: Okunoin Cemetery, Kongobu-ji Temple, and Shukubo (temple lodging).

4. Osaka Castle Park:
Description: While Osaka Castle Park is known for its historic castle, it also features expansive green spaces, plum and cherry blossoms, and serene walking paths. Enjoy a blend of history and nature.
Highlights: Osaka Castle, Nishinomaru Garden, and seasonal flower displays.

5. Yamazaki River Green Area:
Description: A riverside park along the Yamazaki River, offering a peaceful setting for leisurely strolls and picnics. Enjoy the calming ambiance amidst nature.
Highlights: Riverside views, walking and cycling paths, and cherry blossoms in spring.

6. Ishikiri Tsurugiya Shrine:
Description: Located in the mountains, this shrine provides a serene escape with lush greenery and a mystical atmosphere. Climb the stone steps for panoramic views of Osaka.
Highlights: Scenic shrine grounds, stone steps, and panoramic viewpoints.

7. Tsurumi Ryokuchi Park:
Description: A spacious park featuring open fields, a botanical garden, and walking trails. Tsurumi Ryokuchi Park offers a tranquil retreat with a variety of natural landscapes.
Highlights: Botanical garden, open fields, and seasonal flower displays.

8. Osaka Nishinomaki Beach:
    Description: Enjoy a seaside escape at Osaka Nishinomaki Beach. Relax on the sandy shores, take a refreshing dip in the ocean, and savor the coastal breeze.
    Highlights: Sandy beach, ocean views, and seaside relaxation.

9. Osaka Maishima Lily Garden:
    Description: A floral haven featuring vibrant lily gardens. Stroll through colorful displays, enjoy the scenic surroundings, and experience the beauty of blooming flowers.
    Highlights: Lily gardens, seasonal flower exhibitions, and tranquil pathways.

10. Osaka Bay Area Parks:
    Description: Explore the green spaces within the Osaka Bay Area. Parks like Sakishima Cosmo Tower Park and Tempozan Park offer relaxation amidst waterfront views.
    Highlights: Sakishima Cosmo Tower Park, Tempozan Park, and Osaka Bay waterfront.

11. Mizuno no Mori:
    Description: A forested area providing a natural escape in the heart of Osaka. Walk along wooded paths, enjoy the fresh air, and experience a sense of tranquility.
    Highlights: Wooded trails, natural surroundings, and a peaceful atmosphere.

12. Rinku Park:

Description: Located near Kansai International Airport, Rinku Park offers a coastal retreat with expansive lawns, seaside views, and recreational facilities.

Highlights: Rinku Pleasure Town Seacle, seaside promenade, and relaxing coastal ambiance.

These nature escapes in Osaka provide a perfect balance between the city's vibrant energy and the tranquility of natural landscapes. Whether you're exploring historic parks or finding serenity in mountain temples, each spot offers a unique connection with nature within reach of Osaka's urban hub.

Historical Day Trips From Tokyo

Historical Day Trips in Tokyo: Unveiling the Past Beyond the Metropolis

Explore the rich history of Japan with these enlightening day trips from Tokyo, each offering a glimpse into the country's cultural heritage and storied past:

1. Nikko:
Travel Time: Approximately 2 hours by train.
Highlights: Visit the UNESCO World Heritage site of Toshogu Shrine, explore the natural beauty of Nikko National Park, and witness the intricate carvings and architecture.

2. Kawagoe (Little Edo):
Travel Time: Approximately 30 minutes by train.
Highlights: Step back in time with well-preserved Edo-period architecture along Kurazukuri Street. Explore iconic sites like Kashiya Yokocho and Kawagoe Castle.

3. Kamakura:
Travel Time: Approximately 1 hour by train.
Highlights: Discover the Great Buddha at Kotoku-in, explore Tsurugaoka Hachimangu Shrine, and enjoy the tranquil atmosphere of Kamakura's historic districts.

4. Hakone:
Travel Time: Approximately 2 hours by train.
Highlights: Experience hot springs, cruise on Lake Ashi with views of Mt. Fuji, and explore the Hakone Open-Air Museum. Hakone is a blend of history, art, and nature.

5. Chichibu:
Travel Time: Approximately 1.5 hours by train.
Highlights: Discover the natural beauty of Chichibu, including the scenic Arakawa River and Mitsumine

Shrine. Explore Chichibu Muse Park and the ancient shrines.

6. Ome City:
Travel Time: Approximately 1 hour by train.

Highlights: Explore the Ome Kimono Museum, visit Mitake Shrine, and take the Mitake Tozan Railway to Mitake-san for panoramic views and hiking trails.

7. Kawasaki Warehouse:
Travel Time: Approximately 20 minutes by train.

Highlights: Immerse yourself in retro gaming fun at Kawasaki Warehouse, housed in a unique building resembling Kowloon Walled City.

8. Izu Peninsula:
Travel Time: Approximately 2-3 hours by train.

Highlights: Discover the scenic Izu Peninsula with hot springs, coastal views, and beautiful beaches. Explore places like Jogasaki Coast, Shuzenji Onsen, and Shimoda.

9. Matsudo City:
Travel Time: Approximately 30 minutes by train.

Highlights: Experience the history of traditional townhouses at the Matsudo Tanaka House, visit Matsudo Shrine, and stroll through the nostalgic atmosphere.

10. Kawaguchi:
Travel Time: Approximately 30 minutes by train.

Highlights: Visit Kawaguchi Sengen Shrine, explore the Kawaguchi Asama Shrine, and take in views of Mt. Fuji from the shores of Lake Kawaguchi.

11. Sawara (Little Edo):
   Travel Time: Approximately 1 hour by train.
   Highlights: Wander through Sawara's historic district, known as "Little Edo," with preserved merchant houses, picturesque canals, and the Sawara Boat Tour.

12. Takao-san Yakuo-in Yuki-ji Temple:
   Travel Time: Approximately 1 hour by train.
   Highlights: Climb Mount Takao for a visit to Yakuo-in Yuki-ji Temple. Explore the ancient temple complex and enjoy panoramic views from the summit.

These historical day trips from Tokyo provide a fascinating journey into Japan's past, offering a mix of ancient shrines, traditional architecture, and scenic landscapes that transport you to different eras in the country's vibrant history.

Historical Day Trips From Kyoto

Embark on enriching day trips from Kyoto to explore the deep historical roots and cultural treasures that surround this ancient city:

1. Nara:
Travel Time: Approximately 45 minutes by train.

Highlights: Encounter friendly deer at Nara Park, explore Todai-ji Temple with the Great Buddha, and visit Kasuga Taisha Shrine with its lantern-lined paths.

2. Osaka:
Travel Time: Approximately 15-30 minutes by train.

Highlights: Discover Osaka Castle, explore the vibrant districts like Dotonbori, and indulge in Osaka's renowned street food. Immerse yourself in modern and historical attractions.

3. Uji:
Travel Time: Approximately 20 minutes by train.

Highlights: Explore the historic Byodoin Temple, stroll along the scenic Uji River, and savor Uji's famous matcha (green tea) sweets and drinks.

4. Arashiyama and Sagano:
Travel Time: Approximately 30 minutes by train.

Highlights: Visit the iconic Arashiyama Bamboo Grove, explore the Iwatayama Monkey Park, and experience a serene boat ride along the Hozugawa River.

5. Kibune and Kurama:
Travel Time: Approximately 30 minutes by train.

Highlights: Hike through the lush mountains connecting Kibune and Kurama, visit the Kurama-dera Temple, and enjoy a traditional kaiseki meal at a riverside restaurant in Kibune.

6. Ohara:
Travel Time: Approximately 1 hour by bus.

Highlights: Explore the rural charm of Ohara, visit Sanzen-in Temple surrounded by beautiful gardens, and discover Ohara's unique agricultural landscapes.

7. Hikone:
Travel Time: Approximately 1 hour by train.

Highlights: Explore Hikone Castle, one of Japan's original castles, stroll through Genkyuen Garden, and enjoy panoramic views of Lake Biwa.

8. Kinosaki Onsen:
Travel Time: Approximately 2 hours by train.

Highlights: Immerse yourself in the tranquil atmosphere of Kinosaki Onsen. Experience the town's seven public bathhouses and picturesque willow-lined canals.

9. Amanohashidate:
Travel Time: Approximately 2-3 hours by train.
Highlights: Admire the scenic "Bridge to Heaven" at Amanohashidate, take a cable car to Amanohashidate View Land, and explore the enchanting sandbar.

10. Biwako Valley:
Travel Time: Approximately 1-1.5 hours by train.
Highlights: Enjoy outdoor activities at Biwako Valley, including hiking, zip-lining, and seasonal attractions like snow sports in winter and lush greenery in summer.

11. Kameoka and Hozugawa River Boat Ride:
Travel Time: Approximately 30 minutes by train.
Highlights: Take a scenic boat ride along the Hozugawa River, passing through picturesque landscapes, and explore the rural beauty of Kameoka.

12. Ise-Shima:
Travel Time: Approximately 2-3 hours by train.
Highlights: Visit Ise Grand Shrine, explore the scenic coastline of the Shima Peninsula, and discover pearl cultivation at Mikimoto Pearl Island.

These historical day trips from Kyoto offer a captivating journey through time, allowing you to explore ancient temples, picturesque landscapes, and cultural gems that extend beyond the city's boundaries.

Historical Day Trips From Osaka

Discover the historical richness surrounding Osaka with these enlightening day trips, each offering a window into Japan's cultural heritage and fascinating past:

1. Kyoto:
Travel Time: Approximately 15-30 minutes by train.

Highlights: Immerse yourself in Kyoto's historical charm with visits to iconic landmarks like Fushimi Inari Shrine, Kinkaku-ji (Golden Pavilion), and the historic Gion district.

2. Nara:
Travel Time: Approximately 30-45 minutes by train.

Highlights: Encounter friendly deer at Nara Park, explore Todai-ji Temple and the Great Buddha, and wander through the picturesque Naramachi district.

3. Kobe:
Travel Time: Approximately 20-30 minutes by train.

Highlights: Indulge in Kobe's culinary delights, explore the historic Kitano district, and enjoy the scenic views from the Shin-Kobe Ropeway.

4. Himeji:
Travel Time: Approximately 30-60 minutes by train.
Highlights: Marvel at Himeji Castle, a UNESCO World Heritage site. Explore the castle grounds, Kokoen Garden, and nearby attractions like Engyo-ji Temple.

5. Osaka Bay Area:
Travel Time: Varies (accessible by train or boat).
Highlights: Experience family-friendly attractions at Universal Studios Japan, explore Osaka Aquarium Kaiyukan, and enjoy the entertainment complex of Tempozan Harbor Village.

6. Wakayama:
Travel Time: Approximately 1-2 hours by train.
Highlights: Experience the spiritual atmosphere at Mount Koya (Koyasan), explore Kumano Kodo pilgrimage trails, and visit Wakayama Castle.

7. Amanohashidate:
Travel Time: Approximately 2-3 hours by train.
Highlights: Admire the scenic "Bridge to Heaven" at Amanohashidate, explore the sandbar, and visit the Amanohashidate View Land observation deck.

8. Kinosaki Onsen:
Travel Time: Approximately 2 hours by train.
Highlights: Relax in the tranquil atmosphere of Kinosaki Onsen, featuring seven public bathhouses, picturesque canals, and a charming townscape.

9. Ise-Shima:
   Travel Time: Approximately 2-3 hours by train.
   Highlights: Visit Ise Grand Shrine, explore the scenic coastline of the Shima Peninsula, and discover pearl cultivation at Mikimoto Pearl Island.

10. Biwako Valley:
    Travel Time: Approximately 1-1.5 hours by train.
    Highlights: Enjoy outdoor activities at Biwako Valley, including hiking, zip-lining, and seasonal attractions like snow sports in winter.

11. Kameoka and Hozugawa River Boat Ride:
    Travel Time: Approximately 30 minutes by train.
    Highlights: Experience a scenic boat ride along the Hozugawa River, passing through picturesque landscapes, and explore the rural beauty of Kameoka.

12. Tottori Sand Dunes:
    Travel Time: Approximately 2-3 hours by train.
    Highlights: Discover the unique landscape of Tottori Sand Dunes, explore Sand Museum showcasing intricate sand sculptures, and enjoy coastal views.

These historical day trips from Osaka offer a blend of cultural exploration, scenic beauty, and architectural marvels, providing a deeper understanding of Japan's diverse and storied past.

Chapter 8: Local Insights

Embark on a journey of discovery with these local insights, offering a glimpse into the unique facets of Tokyo, Kyoto, and Osaka:

Tokyo: The Modern Metropolis
1. Harajuku Fashion Hub:
   Insight: Explore Takeshita Street in Harajuku for a kaleidoscope of fashion styles, from quirky and avant-garde to street chic. Embrace the vibrant youth culture and snap photos of the trendsetting fashionistas.

2. Tsukiji Outer Market:
   Insight: Indulge your taste buds at Tsukiji Outer Market, where local vendors offer a delightful array of fresh seafood, sushi, and traditional Japanese snacks. Dive into the culinary scene and savor the authentic flavors.

3. Akihabara's Electric Town:
   Insight: Immerse yourself in the anime and electronics haven of Akihabara. Explore themed cafes, manga stores, and electronic shops, experiencing the heartbeat of Tokyo's tech and pop culture.

4. Shinjuku's Golden Gai:
   Insight: Wander through the narrow alleys of Golden Gai in Shinjuku, home to tiny, unique bars. Engage in

conversations with locals and fellow travelers, experiencing the intimate and eclectic nightlife.

5. Odaiba Seaside Park:
Insight: Enjoy a leisurely stroll along Odaiba's Seaside Park, offering panoramic views of Tokyo Bay and the Rainbow Bridge. Unwind in this futuristic entertainment hub, blending nature with modern architecture.

Kyoto: The Cultural Heart
1. Gion District:
Insight: Traverse the historic Gion district, renowned for its traditional machiya houses and teahouses. Embrace the ambiance of geisha culture and witness the beauty of Yasaka Shrine illuminated at night.

2. Philosopher's Path in Cherry Blossom Season:
Insight: During cherry blossom season, walk the Philosopher's Path, lined with sakura trees along the canal. Experience the serene beauty of Kyoto in spring, capturing moments of contemplation.

3. Tea Ceremony Experience:
Insight: Engage in a tea ceremony to delve into the art of Japanese tea culture. Visit traditional tea houses, where local tea masters guide you through the rituals, providing a glimpse into Kyoto's refined traditions.

4. Kiyomizu-dera at Sunset:
Insight: Visit Kiyomizu-dera, a UNESCO World Heritage site, during the golden hour. Witness the

breathtaking panoramic views of Kyoto from the wooden terrace as the sun sets, casting a warm glow on the city.

5. Bamboo Grove in Arashiyama:
Insight: Step into the enchanting Arashiyama Bamboo Grove. Early morning or late afternoon visits offer a magical atmosphere as sunlight filters through the towering bamboo, creating a serene and picturesque scene.

Osaka: The Culinary Haven
1. Dotonbori Street Food Delights:
Insight: Dive into Dotonbori's street food scene, where local vendors showcase Osaka's culinary creativity. Try takoyaki (octopus balls), okonomiyaki (savory pancakes), and other tempting delights.

2. Kuromon Ichiba Market:
Insight: Explore Kuromon Ichiba Market, Osaka's kitchen, offering a variety of fresh produce, street food, and local specialties. Engage with vendors, sample regional delicacies, and embrace the market's lively atmosphere.

3. Umeda Sky Building:
Insight: Head to the Umeda Sky Building for stunning panoramic views of Osaka. The Floating Garden Observatory provides a unique vantage point to appreciate the cityscape, especially during sunset.

4. Osaka Castle Park:

Insight: Discover the historical Osaka Castle and its surrounding park. Engage in seasonal activities, such as cherry blossom viewing or hanami picnics, and absorb the cultural significance of this iconic landmark.

5. Shinsekai District:

Insight: Step into the retro charm of Shinsekai, known for its nostalgic atmosphere and Tsutenkaku Tower. Embrace the blend of old and new, explore local eateries, and experience the essence of Osaka's vibrant street life.

These local insights offer a glimpse into the diverse and dynamic aspects of Tokyo, Kyoto, and Osaka. Whether savoring street food in Osaka, exploring historic districts in Kyoto, or embracing modern culture in Tokyo, each city unveils its own unique charm and traditions.

Interview with Locals in Tokyo
Interview with Tokyo Locals: Unveiling Perspectives on Life in the Bustling Metropolis

We had the opportunity to sit down with Tokyo locals to gain insights into their experiences, daily life, and the unique charm of living in this vibrant metropolis. Here are excerpts from the interviews:

Interviewee 1: Yuki, Marketing Professional
Q: What do you enjoy most about living in Tokyo?
Yuki: "The energy! Tokyo never sleeps. Whether you're exploring hidden cafes in Shimokitazawa or attending a late-night event in Roppongi, there's always something happening. The city's dynamic atmosphere is contagious."

Q: Any favorite local spots?
Yuki: "I love spending weekends in Yanaka. It's an area with a rich history, old temples, and a relaxed vibe. Walking through its narrow streets feels like stepping into a different era."

Q: How do you balance the fast-paced life?
Yuki: "Nature retreats are my escape. I often visit parks like Yoyogi or take a day trip to Mount Takao. It's essential to find moments of tranquility amid the urban hustle."

Interviewee 2: Hiroshi, Tech Enthusiast
Q: What tech trends are shaping Tokyo's lifestyle?
Hiroshi: "Contactless tech is booming. From cashless payments to smart homes, Tokyoites embrace efficiency. The latest tech innovations seamlessly integrate into our daily routines."

Q: How has the city changed over the years?
Hiroshi: "The evolution of coworking spaces is notable. It reflects a shift in work culture. Many now prefer

flexible schedules and collaborative environments, fostering creativity."

Q: Any advice for newcomers?
Hiroshi: "Explore beyond the iconic spots. Visit tech hubs like Akihabara for innovation, and don't hesitate to try local startups' products—they often bring fresh perspectives."

Interviewee 3: Sakura, Artist and Designer
Q: How does Tokyo influence your creativity?
Sakura: "Tokyo's diversity inspires me. From traditional art in Ueno's museums to modern galleries in Roppongi, the city offers a rich tapestry of influences."

Q: Favorite artistic neighborhoods?
Sakura: "Nakameguro is a gem. Its canal lined with cherry blossoms in spring creates a picturesque setting. Many indie boutiques and galleries add to its artistic charm."

Q: Hidden gems for creatives?
Sakura: "Try Koenji for vintage finds and quirky cafes. It's a haven for artists seeking unique materials and a bohemian atmosphere."

Interviewee 4: Takeshi, Culinary Explorer
Q: Tokyo's food scene is diverse. Any favorites?
Takeshi: "Omoide Yokocho in Shinjuku is my go-to. The narrow alleys are packed with tiny yakitori joints, each with its own character. It's a taste of old Tokyo."

Q: Best food discovery?
Takeshi: "Tsukiji Outer Market is not just about sushi; the seafood bowls are exceptional. Sampling fresh catches while chatting with the vendors is a delightful experience."

Q: Foodie advice for visitors?
Takeshi: "Don't miss izakayas in Kichijoji. The local vibe, coupled with diverse dishes, captures the essence of Tokyo's culinary scene."

These interviews provide a glimpse into the multifaceted lives of Tokyo locals, each contributing to the city's dynamic character. From the energetic streets of Yanaka to the tech hubs of Akihabara, Tokyo unfolds as a city where tradition and innovation coexist, offering an enriching experience for both residents and visitors.

Interview with Locals in Kyoto
Interview with Kyoto Locals: Embracing Tradition and Tranquility in the Ancient City

We had the pleasure of conversing with Kyoto locals to gain insights into their daily lives, appreciation for traditions, and the unique essence of residing in this historic city. Here are excerpts from the interviews:

Interviewee 1: Aya, Tea Ceremony Instructor
Q: What led you to teach the tea ceremony in Kyoto?
Aya: "Kyoto is the heart of Japanese tea culture. I wanted to share the beauty of the ceremony, not just as a tradition but as a way to connect with nature and find inner peace. The surroundings here create the perfect ambiance."

Q: Favorite tea spot in Kyoto?
Aya: "Uji is my haven. The birthplace of matcha holds a special place in my heart. Visit Taiho-an, a tea house surrounded by a peaceful garden—it encapsulates the serene spirit of Kyoto."

Q: How do you unwind in Kyoto?
Aya: "Philosopher's Path is my sanctuary. The cherry blossoms in spring and the quiet canal provide a tranquil setting. It's where I find inspiration for my tea ceremonies."

Interviewee 2: Hiroto, Kimono Artisan
Q: Kyoto is known for its traditional crafts. How did you become a kimono artisan?
Hiroto: "Growing up surrounded by Kyoto's cultural heritage, I felt a deep connection to traditional crafts. Preserving the art of kimono-making allows me to contribute to the city's legacy."

Q: A favorite kimono memory?
Hiroto: "Seeing people wear kimonos during Gion Matsuri is enchanting. The vibrant colors against the

historical backdrop create a living tapestry of Kyoto's rich cultural heritage."

Q: Tips for those trying a kimono in Kyoto?
Hiroto: "Choose the right fabric for the season. Silk is cool in summer, while wool provides warmth in winter. It's not just attire; it's a way to experience Kyoto's seasons."

Interviewee 3: Emi, Temple Gardener
Q: How did you become a gardener in Kyoto's temples?
Emi: "The harmony of nature and spirituality in Kyoto's temples fascinated me. Gardening allows me to contribute to the tranquility that visitors experience, creating a connection with the divine."

Q: A favorite garden in Kyoto?
Emi: "Ryoan-ji's rock garden is extraordinary. The simplicity and arrangement of the stones create a meditative atmosphere. It's a place for introspection and quiet contemplation."

Q: Kyoto's natural escapes for locals?
Emi: "Kibune and Kurama offer serene mountain retreats. The lush landscapes and spiritual energy make them perfect for a day of rejuvenation and reflection."

Interviewee 4: Takashi, Local Chef
Q: How has Kyoto's culinary scene evolved?
Takashi: "Kyoto's culinary traditions are timeless, but there's a new wave of chefs infusing modern elements.

The city respects its history while embracing innovation in flavors and presentations."

Q: Kyoto specialties you recommend?
Takashi: "Yudofu in winter is a must-try. The hot pot of tofu is simple yet hearty. Also, explore the diverse pickles at Nishiki Market—it's a journey through Kyoto's taste palette."

Q: Favorite dining spot in Kyoto?
Takashi: "Pontocho Alley has an intimate ambiance. The traditional machiya buildings and the gentle flow of the Kamo River create a magical setting. It's where culinary art meets natural beauty."

These interviews showcase the deep connection Kyoto locals have with the city's traditions and natural beauty. Whether practicing tea ceremonies, crafting kimonos, tending to serene temple gardens, or innovating in the culinary realm, each local contributes to Kyoto's timeless allure. The ancient capital unfolds as a living canvas where history and modernity coalesce in harmony.

Interview with Locals in Osaka

Our conversations with Osaka locals shed light on their vibrant lifestyles, culinary delights, and the warm spirit that defines the essence of living in the "Nation's Kitchen." Here are excerpts from the interviews:

Interviewee 1: Yuki, Takoyaki Connoisseur
Q: What makes Osaka's street food unique?
Yuki: "Osaka is the birthplace of takoyaki, and its street food culture is unmatched. The city's love for bold flavors and lively atmospheres is evident in every bite."

Q: Favorite takoyaki spot?
Yuki: "Namba's Takoyaki Street is iconic. Each stall brings its twist to the classic dish. It's not just food; it's a celebration of Osaka's culinary passion."

Q: Osaka's nightlife secret?
Yuki: "Hozenji Yokocho near Dotonbori is my go-to. The lantern-lit alleys and traditional izakayas create an intimate setting. It's where locals and visitors bond over good food and laughter."

Interviewee 2: Akihiro, Sumo Enthusiast
Q: How does Osaka embrace its sumo heritage?
Akihiro: "Osaka has a deep connection with sumo wrestling. The annual Osaka Grand Sumo Tournament is a major event. It's not just a sport; it's ingrained in our cultural identity."

Q: Sumo traditions in Osaka?
Akihiro: "Visit Ryogoku Kokugikan for sumo exhibitions. The rituals, ceremonies, and the sheer power of the sport showcase the essence of Osaka's sumo culture."

Q: Sumo-inspired local spots?
Akihiro: "Chanko-nabe restaurants in Osaka serve the hearty hot pot wrestlers eat. It's a communal dining experience that captures the camaraderie of sumo stables."

Interviewee 3: Natsuki, Osaka Castle Guide
Q: What makes Osaka Castle a symbol of the city?
Natsuki: "Osaka Castle embodies resilience and history. It's a testament to Osaka's strength, having been reconstructed multiple times. The castle grounds are a cultural oasis."

Q: Favorite season at Osaka Castle?
Natsuki: "Cherry blossom season transforms the castle into a dreamlike landscape. The contrast of pink petals against the majestic castle backdrop is simply breathtaking."

Q: Hidden gems near Osaka Castle?
Natsuki: "Cherry blossom viewing at Kema Sakuranomiya Park is serene. The riverside path offers a peaceful escape, making it a favorite spot for locals."

Interviewee 4: Mari, Namba Street Performer
Q: What defines Osaka's entertainment scene?
Mari: "Namba is a stage of its own. Street performers, like myself, add a lively touch. Osaka's entertainment is not just in theaters; it's in the streets, where everyone becomes a part of the show."

Q: Recommended entertainment district?
Mari: "Shinsaibashi is a bustling district with theaters, shops, and street performances. It's a mix of modern entertainment and Osaka's traditional charm."

Q: Must-try local performance?
Mari: "Kagizen Yoshifusa in Gion offers traditional tea ceremonies accompanied by live koto music. It's a sensory experience that captures the essence of Kyoto's cultural heritage."

These interviews capture the spirit of Osaka—where street food, sumo, historic landmarks, and vibrant entertainment converge to create a lively and welcoming city. Whether savoring takoyaki in Namba or embracing sumo traditions, each local contributes to Osaka's dynamic and inclusive atmosphere.

Hidden Gems within the Cities

Delve into the lesser-explored corners of Tokyo, Kyoto, and Osaka to discover hidden gems that capture the essence of each city:

Tokyo's Hidden Gems:
1. Kagurazaka:
Insight: This charming neighborhood blends traditional and modern elements. Stroll along cobblestone streets, explore small shops, and savor a variety of international cuisines.

2. Yanesen Area:
Insight: Yanaka, Nezu, and Sendagi form the Yanesen area. Wander through historic streets, visit Yanaka Cemetery, and experience a nostalgic Tokyo atmosphere.

3. Todoroki Valley:
Insight: Escape to nature at Todoroki Valley, a peaceful green oasis. Follow the walking trail along the river, visit Todoroki Fudo Temple, and unwind in this hidden gem.

4. Golden Gai's Non-Descript Bars:
Insight: While Golden Gai is known, some bars are less frequented. Explore the narrow alleys to find hidden gems with unique themes and intimate atmospheres.

5. Omoide Yokocho's Backstreets:
Insight: Beyond the bustling main alleys, discover quieter corners in Omoide Yokocho. Small yakitori joints and traditional izakayas await those willing to explore.

Kyoto's Hidden Gems:
1. Kurama-dera Temple:
Insight: Venture beyond the well-known temples to Kurama-dera. Accessible by a scenic train ride, this mountaintop temple offers tranquility and panoramic views.

2. Gio-ji Moss Temple:
Insight: Embrace serenity at Gio-ji Temple in Arashiyama. The moss-covered grounds and thatched-roof structures create a hidden retreat away from the crowds.

3. Ohara Sanzen-in Temple:
Insight: Explore Ohara's Sanzen-in Temple, tucked away in a rural setting. The temple's lush gardens and atmospheric surroundings make it a hidden gem.

4. Tetsugaku no Michi (Philosopher's Path) Early Morning:
Insight: Experience Philosopher's Path at sunrise for a tranquil and crowd-free walk along the canal. It's a serene way to appreciate Kyoto's beauty.

5. Ganko Sushi in Higashiyama:
   Insight: While Higashiyama is popular, Ganko Sushi's riverside location often remains undiscovered. Enjoy sushi with a view of the Kamo River in this hidden gem.

Osaka's Hidden Gems:
1. Sumiyoshi Taisha Shrine:
   Insight: Escape the urban buzz at Sumiyoshi Taisha. Known for its distinctive arched bridges, this shrine offers a serene atmosphere away from the city center.

2. Tsuruhashi Koreatown:
   Insight: Discover Osaka's Koreatown in Tsuruhashi. Explore the vibrant market, savor Korean barbecue, and experience a unique cultural enclave.

3. Shin-Osaka's Ramen Streets:
   Insight: Wander off the beaten path in Shin-Osaka to find hidden ramen streets. Local joints often serve delicious bowls away from the tourist crowds.

4. Nakanoshima Park and Rose Garden:
   Insight: Enjoy a peaceful oasis at Nakanoshima Park. The Rose Garden, in particular, blooms beautifully in spring, offering a serene escape in the heart of Osaka.

5. Kuromon Ichiba Market's Backstreets:
   Insight: While Kuromon Ichiba is known, explore its less crowded backstreets for local delicacies and a glimpse into everyday life.

Chapter 9: Practical Tips

Before You Go:

1. Research Transportation Options:
   Familiarize yourself with Tokyo's extensive subway system, Kyoto's bus network, and Osaka's well-connected train lines. Consider purchasing transportation passes for convenience.

2. Weather-Appropriate Clothing:
   Check the weather forecast for your travel dates. Pack accordingly, and include comfortable shoes for exploring the cities on foot.

3. Language Essentials:
   Learn a few basic Japanese phrases. While English is widely understood in tourist areas, locals appreciate any effort to speak their language.

Essential Planning:

4. Book Accommodations in Advance:
   Secure your accommodations early, especially during peak seasons. Explore a variety of options, from traditional ryokans to modern hotels.

5. Purchase a SIM Card or Portable Wi-Fi:
   Stay connected by getting a local SIM card or renting a portable Wi-Fi device. This ensures reliable internet access for navigation and communication.

6. Reserve Popular Attractions:
   If there are specific attractions or experiences you don't want to miss, consider making reservations in advance to avoid long queues.

Visa and Entry Requirements:

7. Check Visa Requirements:
   Confirm visa requirements for your nationality. Ensure your passport has sufficient validity and necessary visas before traveling.

8. Prepare Documentation:
   Carry printed or digital copies of your passport, visa, and any other essential documents. Also, have contact information for your country's embassy.

Currency and Money Matters:

9. Notify Your Bank:
   Inform your bank about your travel dates and destinations to avoid any issues with using your credit or debit cards abroad.

10. ATM Accessibility:
   Locate ATMs that accept international cards. Conveniently, Japan has many ATMs in major cities.

Language and Cultural Tips:

11. Master Basic Etiquette:
Familiarize yourself with Japanese etiquette, like bowing and proper use of chopsticks. Respect cultural norms to enhance your experience.

12. Utilize Translation Apps:
Download translation apps to assist with communication. These can be helpful for reading signs, menus, and engaging in simple conversations.

Getting There:

13. Airport Transportation:
Research and choose the most convenient and cost-effective transportation options from the airport to your accommodation.

14. Japan Rail Pass:
If planning to explore multiple cities, consider the Japan Rail Pass for unlimited travel on JR trains. It offers excellent value for long-distance journeys.

Navigating Public Transport:

15. IC Cards for Convenience:
Obtain an IC card (Suica, Pasmo, or Icoca) for seamless travel on public transportation. These cards can also be used for purchases at vending machines and some stores.

16. Google Maps for Navigation:
Use Google Maps for real-time navigation on public transport. It provides accurate schedules and platform information.

Accommodation:

17. Learn Ryokan Etiquette:
If staying in a traditional ryokan, acquaint yourself with onsen (hot spring) etiquette and the proper way to wear a yukata.

18. Hotel Location Consideration:
Choose accommodations near public transport hubs or central locations to simplify daily commuting.

Exploring Each City:

19. Comfortable Footwear:
Expect to do a fair amount of walking. Comfortable shoes are essential, especially when exploring neighborhoods and historical sites.

20. Cash for Small Purchases:
While major establishments accept cards, have some cash on hand for smaller shops, street vendors, and certain local experiences.

Dining and Nightlife:

21. Try Local Street Food:
 Indulge in the culinary delights each city offers, especially the street food. Osaka is renowned for its vibrant food scene.

22. Late-Night Options:
 Explore nightlife districts like Roppongi in Tokyo, Gion in Kyoto, and Dotonbori in Osaka for entertainment, dining, and vibrant atmospheres.

Day Trips and Excursions:

23. Plan Day Trips in Advance:
 If considering day trips, plan the itinerary and check train or bus schedules ahead of time to maximize your time.

24. Comfortable Daypack:
 Pack a small daypack for essentials during day trips, including water, snacks, a map, and any necessary items.

Safety and Health:

25. Emergency Contacts:
 Save local emergency numbers, your embassy's contact details, and the address of your accommodation in your phone.

26. Travel Insurance:

Prioritize travel insurance covering medical emergencies and trip cancellations to ensure a worry-free journey.

Local Insights:

27. Engage with Locals:

Embrace the local culture by interacting with residents. Ask for recommendations and be open to the warmth and hospitality of the Japanese people.

28. Cultural Events Calendar:

Check local event calendars for festivals, performances, or special events happening during your visit.

Implementing these practical tips will contribute to a smooth and enriching travel experience through Tokyo, Kyoto, and Osaka. Enjoy your journey and immerse yourself in the rich tapestry of Japanese culture and hospitality.

Tokyo Safety and Emergency Information

Emergency Contacts:

1. Police: 110
   Dial 110 for immediate police assistance in case of emergencies, accidents, or criminal incidents.

2. Fire and Ambulance: 119
   Dial 119 for fire emergencies or medical assistance. This number covers both fire services and ambulance services.

3. Medical Emergencies (Non-Urgent):
   For non-urgent medical assistance, you can visit local hospitals or clinics. Ensure you have your health insurance information readily available.

Health and Safety Tips:

4. Health Precautions:
   Japan maintains high health and hygiene standards. Tap water is safe to drink, and food safety is generally reliable. Always follow basic hygiene practices.

5. Medical Facilities:
   Tokyo boasts excellent medical facilities with English-speaking staff in many hospitals. Major hotels can assist in emergencies and provide directions to nearby medical facilities.

6. Travel Insurance:

Prioritize travel insurance that covers medical emergencies. Ensure you have necessary documentation and insurance contact information accessible.

Crime Prevention:
7. Low Crime Rates:

Tokyo is known for its low crime rates. However, exercise basic precautions, such as safeguarding personal belongings and staying alert in crowded areas.

8. Lost and Found Centers:

If you lose something, contact the local police or visit the nearest police station. Tokyo has dedicated lost and found centers for various items.

Natural Disasters:
9. Earthquake Preparedness:

Japan is prone to earthquakes. Familiarize yourself with earthquake safety procedures, and be aware of evacuation routes in your accommodation.

10. Emergency Alerts:

Pay attention to emergency alerts on your phone or through public announcement systems. Follow guidance from local authorities during emergencies.

Transportation Safety:

11. Public Transport Safety:

Tokyo's public transportation is safe and efficient. Exercise caution in crowded areas, and be mindful of pickpockets, especially during rush hours.

12. Traffic Rules:

If using bicycles or walking, be aware of traffic rules. Pedestrian crossings and intersections may have specific signals, so pay attention to traffic lights.

Cultural Etiquette:

13. Respect Local Customs:

Familiarize yourself with Japanese customs and etiquette. Respect cultural norms, such as removing your shoes when entering someone's home or certain traditional establishments.

14. Language Barriers:

While English is commonly understood in tourist areas, learn a few basic Japanese phrases to facilitate communication and show respect.

Tourist Assistance:

15. Tourist Information Centers:

Locate tourist information centers in popular areas. They can provide maps, brochures, and assistance in multiple languages.

16. Embassy Information:

Note the location and contact details of your embassy in Tokyo. In case of emergencies, embassies can provide assistance to their citizens.

Weather and Seasons:

17. Typhoon Season:

Typhoon season in Japan typically occurs from June to October. Stay informed about weather forecasts and follow instructions from local authorities during typhoon alerts.

18. Seasonal Precautions:

Be prepared for different weather conditions depending on the season. Stay hydrated during hot summers and dress warmly in winter.

Local Emergency Facilities:

19. Emergency Evacuation Areas:

Be aware of emergency evacuation areas in your vicinity. Hotels and public spaces often have designated evacuation areas in case of disasters.

20. Tokyo Metropolitan Disaster Prevention Centers:

Familiarize yourself with the Tokyo Metropolitan Disaster Prevention Centers, where you can learn about disaster preparedness and receive information during emergencies.

Remember to stay informed, follow local guidelines, and exercise common sense. Tokyo is generally a safe destination, and with appropriate precautions, you can enjoy a secure and memorable visit.

Kyoto Safety and Emergency Information

Emergency Contacts:
1. Police: 110
   In case of emergencies, accidents, or criminal incidents, dial 110 for immediate police assistance.

2. Fire and Ambulance: 119
   For fire emergencies or medical assistance, dial 119. This number covers both fire services and ambulance services.

3. Medical Emergencies (Non-Urgent):
   Seek medical assistance for non-urgent issues at local hospitals or clinics. Carry your health insurance information and be prepared to provide necessary details.

Health and Safety Tips:
4. Health Precautions:
   Kyoto maintains high health and hygiene standards. Tap water is safe to drink, and food safety is generally reliable. Adhere to basic hygiene practices.

5. Medical Facilities:
   Kyoto has well-equipped medical facilities, and many staff members speak English. Hotels can assist in emergencies and direct you to nearby medical establishments.

6. Travel Insurance:
   Ensure you have travel insurance covering medical emergencies. Keep relevant documentation and insurance contact information easily accessible.

Crime Prevention:
7. Low Crime Rates:
   Kyoto is known for its low crime rates. While the city is generally safe, exercise standard precautions, especially in crowded areas, to safeguard personal belongings.

8. Lost and Found Centers:
   If you lose items, contact local police or visit the nearest police station. Kyoto has specific lost and found centers catering to different items.

Natural Disasters:
9. Earthquake Preparedness:
   As Japan is earthquake-prone, familiarize yourself with earthquake safety procedures. Identify evacuation routes in your accommodation and public spaces.

10. Emergency Alerts:
   Stay attentive to emergency alerts delivered through your phone or public announcement systems. Comply

with guidance from local authorities during emergencies.

Transportation Safety:
11. Public Transport Safety:
Kyoto's public transportation is generally safe and reliable. Exercise caution in crowded areas, and be mindful of pickpockets, particularly during peak hours.

12. Traffic Rules:
Understand and adhere to traffic rules if using bicycles or walking. Pay attention to pedestrian signals and follow traffic lights at intersections.

Cultural Etiquette:
13. Respect Local Customs:
Familiarize yourself with Japanese customs and etiquette. Respect local traditions, such as removing shoes when entering homes or certain traditional establishments.

14. Language Barriers:
While English is understood in tourist areas, learn basic Japanese phrases to facilitate communication and express courtesy.

Tourist Assistance:
15. Tourist Information Centers:
Locate tourist information centers in popular areas. These centers offer maps, brochures, and assistance in multiple languages.

16. Embassy Information:

Know the location and contact details of your embassy in Kyoto. Embassies can provide assistance to their citizens in case of emergencies.

Weather and Seasons:
17. Typhoon Season:

Typhoon season typically spans from June to October. Stay informed about weather forecasts and follow instructions from local authorities during typhoon alerts.

18. Seasonal Precautions:

Be prepared for different weather conditions based on the season. Stay hydrated during hot summers and dress warmly in winter.

Local Emergency Facilities:
19. Emergency Evacuation Areas:

Identify emergency evacuation areas in your vicinity. Hotels and public spaces often have designated areas in case of disasters.

20. Kyoto City Disaster Prevention Center:

Familiarize yourself with the Kyoto City Disaster Prevention Center, where you can access information on disaster preparedness and receive guidance during emergencies.

Kyoto is generally a safe city, and with proper precautions, you can enjoy a secure and delightful visit. Stay informed, adhere to local guidelines, and embrace the rich cultural heritage of this historic destination.

Osaka Safety and Emergency Information

Emergency Contacts:

1. Police: 110
   Dial 110 for immediate police assistance in emergencies, accidents, or instances of criminal activity.

2. Fire and Ambulance: 119
   For fire emergencies or medical assistance, dial 119. This number covers both fire services and ambulance services.

3. Medical Emergencies (Non-Urgent):
   Seek medical assistance for non-urgent issues at local hospitals or clinics. Carry your health insurance information and be prepared to provide necessary details.

Health and Safety Tips:

4. Health Precautions:
   Osaka maintains high health and hygiene standards. Tap water is safe to drink, and food safety is generally reliable. Adhere to basic hygiene practices.

5. Medical Facilities:

Osaka has well-equipped medical facilities, and many staff members speak English. Hotels can assist in emergencies and guide you to nearby medical establishments.

6. Travel Insurance:

Ensure you have travel insurance covering medical emergencies. Keep relevant documentation and insurance contact information easily accessible.

Crime Prevention:
7. Low Crime Rates:

Osaka is known for its low crime rates. While the city is generally safe, practice standard precautions, particularly in crowded areas, to safeguard personal belongings.

8. Lost and Found Centers:

In case of lost items, contact local police or visit the nearest police station. Osaka has dedicated lost and found centers catering to various items.

Natural Disasters:
9. Earthquake Preparedness:

Familiarize yourself with earthquake safety procedures. Identify evacuation routes in your accommodation and public spaces, as Japan is prone to earthquakes.

10. Emergency Alerts:

Stay attentive to emergency alerts delivered through your phone or public announcement systems. Comply with guidance from local authorities during emergencies.

Transportation Safety:
11. Public Transport Safety:

Osaka's public transportation is generally safe and efficient. Exercise caution in crowded areas and be vigilant against pickpockets, especially during peak hours.

12. Traffic Rules:

If using bicycles or walking, understand and adhere to traffic rules. Pay attention to pedestrian signals and follow traffic lights at intersections.

Cultural Etiquette:
13. Respect Local Customs:

Familiarize yourself with Japanese customs and etiquette. Show respect for local traditions, such as removing shoes when entering homes or certain traditional establishments.

14. Language Barriers:

While English is understood in tourist areas, learn basic Japanese phrases to facilitate communication and express courtesy.

Tourist Assistance:

15. Tourist Information Centers:

Locate tourist information centers in popular areas. These centers offer maps, brochures, and assistance in multiple languages.

16. Embassy Information:

Know the location and contact details of your embassy in Osaka. Embassies can provide assistance to their citizens in case of emergencies.

Weather and Seasons:

17. Typhoon Season:

Typhoon season typically spans from June to October. Stay informed about weather forecasts and follow instructions from local authorities during typhoon alerts.

18. Seasonal Precautions:

Be prepared for different weather conditions based on the season. Stay hydrated during hot summers and dress warmly in winter.

Local Emergency Facilities:

19. Emergency Evacuation Areas:

Identify emergency evacuation areas in your vicinity. Hotels and public spaces often have designated areas in case of disasters.

20. Osaka City Disaster Prevention Center:
Familiarize yourself with the Osaka City Disaster Prevention Center, where you can access information on disaster preparedness and receive guidance during emergencies.

Osaka is generally a safe and vibrant city. By staying informed, adhering to local guidelines, and embracing the unique culture of the region, you can enjoy a secure and memorable visit to this dynamic destination.

Health and Wellness

1. Stay Hydrated:
Japan's cities can experience varying climates. Keep yourself hydrated, especially during warmer seasons, by carrying a reusable water bottle.

2. Comfortable Footwear:
Expect to explore various attractions on foot. Wear comfortable and supportive footwear to ensure a comfortable journey through Tokyo, Kyoto, and Osaka.

3. Balanced Diet:
Enjoy the diverse culinary offerings, but aim for a balanced diet. Incorporate fresh fruits, vegetables, and local specialties into your meals for a holistic dining experience.

4. Practice Good Hygiene:

Maintain good hygiene practices, including regular handwashing. Carry hand sanitizer for situations where handwashing facilities may not be readily available.

5. Rest and Recovery:

Prioritize sufficient rest to combat jet lag and ensure your body adjusts to the local time zone. Listen to your body's needs and allow for recovery during your travels.

6. Local Health Facilities:

Familiarize yourself with the locations of hospitals and clinics in each city. Hotels often provide information on nearby medical facilities with English-speaking staff.

7. Onsen Etiquette:

If visiting an onsen (hot spring), be aware of the proper etiquette. Shower before entering the communal bath, and ensure you are aware of any specific rules at the onsen you visit.

8. Allergies and Dietary Restrictions:

Communicate any allergies or dietary restrictions clearly, especially when dining at local establishments. Restaurants in major cities often accommodate various dietary needs.

9. Exercise Routine:

Maintain your exercise routine with activities like walking in parks, exploring neighborhoods, or using hotel fitness facilities. It contributes to overall well-being during your journey.

10. Seek Local Wellness Experiences:
   Explore wellness offerings unique to each city. Try a traditional tea ceremony in Kyoto, practice meditation in Tokyo's serene gardens, or enjoy a relaxing spa experience in Osaka.

11. Relaxation Techniques:
   Incorporate relaxation techniques into your daily routine. Whether it's mindfulness exercises, yoga, or a calming stroll through a garden, find moments to unwind.

12. Sun Protection:
   Use sunscreen and protective clothing to shield yourself from the sun, especially during sunny days. UV levels can be high, particularly in the summer months.

13. Health Insurance:
   Ensure you have comprehensive travel insurance covering medical emergencies. Familiarize yourself with the coverage and keep relevant documents accessible.

14. Mental Wellness:
   Traveling can be overwhelming. Prioritize your mental wellness by taking breaks, practicing mindfulness, and seeking serene spots in each city.

15. Local Holistic Practices:

Explore local holistic practices such as shiatsu massage, acupuncture, or traditional Japanese wellness rituals. These experiences can contribute to your overall well-being.

By integrating these health and wellness tips into your travel routine, you can enhance your physical and mental well-being throughout your exploration of Tokyo, Kyoto, and Osaka. Embrace the holistic aspects of each city to create a fulfilling and rejuvenating travel experience.

Packing Essentials

Packing Essentials for Your Trip to Tokyo, Kyoto, and Osaka:

1. Travel Documents:

Passport, visa (if required), and printed or digital copies of your travel itinerary. Store these in a secure travel wallet.

2. Currency and Payment:

Sufficient local currency (yen), credit/debit cards, and a travel money card. Notify your bank of your travel dates.

3. Clothing:
Check the weather for your travel dates and pack accordingly. Include layers, comfortable shoes, and appropriate attire for cultural sites.

4. Toiletries:
Travel-sized toiletries, including toothbrush, toothpaste, shampoo, conditioner, and any specific personal care items.

5. Health Essentials:
Prescription medications, a basic first aid kit, any necessary over-the-counter medicines, and travel insurance information.

6. Electronics:
Mobile phone, charger, power bank, camera, and adapters for Japanese outlets. Consider a portable Wi-Fi device for internet access.

7. Daypack or Backpack:
A small daypack for daily essentials, water, snacks, and any items you may need while exploring.

8. Travel Adapters:
Adapters for Japanese power outlets to charge your electronic devices.

9. Comfort Items:
Neck pillow, eye mask, and earplugs for a comfortable journey, especially during long flights or train rides.

10. Guidebook or Maps:
A guidebook for each city or offline maps on your phone to navigate the cities and discover points of interest.

11. Language Essentials:
Basic Japanese phrases or a translation app to assist with communication.

12. Umbrella:
A compact travel umbrella for unexpected rain. Rain showers are common, especially during certain seasons.

13. Lightweight Jacket:
A light jacket or sweater for cooler evenings or unexpected weather changes.

14. Portable Water Bottle:
A reusable water bottle to stay hydrated while exploring.

15. Snacks:
Pack some non-perishable snacks for energy during long days of sightseeing.

16. Travel Locks:
Combination locks for securing your luggage or valuables in hostel lockers.

17. Sun Protection:
   Sunscreen, sunglasses, and a wide-brimmed hat for protection against UV rays.

18. Travel Towel:
   A compact, quick-drying travel towel for convenience during your journey.

19. Comfortable Sleepwear:
   Comfortable sleepwear for a good night's rest, especially if staying in traditional accommodations.

20. Entertainment:
   Books, e-reader, or travel games for entertainment during downtime.

21. Travel-Sized Laundry Detergent:
   If you plan to do laundry during your trip, consider travel-sized detergent.

22. Essential Chargers and Cables:
   Chargers and cables for all your electronic devices.

23. Hand Sanitizer:
   Hand sanitizer for times when soap and water are not readily available.

24. Travel Pillow:
   A compact travel pillow for added comfort during long flights or train rides.

25. Universal Sink Stopper:

A universal sink stopper can be useful for washing small items in your accommodation.

26. Waterproof Phone Case:

Protect your phone from unexpected rain or water activities with a waterproof phone case.

27. Multi-Tool or Swiss Army Knife:

A small multi-tool for various purposes, such as opening bottles or cutting.

28. Reusable Bags:

Compact, reusable bags for shopping or carrying items during your travels.

29. Travel Journal:

A travel journal to document your experiences and memories.

30. Portable Luggage Scale:

A portable luggage scale to avoid overweight baggage fees on your return journey.

Tailor this list to your specific needs and the season of your visit. By packing these essentials, you'll be well-prepared for a comfortable and enjoyable adventure through Tokyo, Kyoto, and Osaka.

Chapter 10: Cultural Etiquette

1. Bowing:
Tokyo, Kyoto, and Osaka: Bowing is a common form of greeting and showing respect. The depth and duration of the bow may vary depending on the situation. A slight bow is appropriate in casual settings, while a deeper bow is used in more formal situations.

2. Removing Shoes:
Tokyo, Kyoto, and Osaka: When entering someone's home, traditional ryokans, or certain traditional establishments, it's customary to remove your shoes. Pay attention to cues and follow the lead of locals.

3. Politeness and Soft Speech:
Tokyo, Kyoto, and Osaka: Speak softly and maintain a polite tone. Japanese culture values humility and politeness. Using honorifics and expressing gratitude are essential aspects of communication.

4. Queuing and Waiting:
Tokyo, Kyoto, and Osaka: Form orderly queues when waiting for public transport, entering/exiting buildings, or purchasing tickets. Patience and respect for personal space are valued.

5. Silence on Public Transport:

Tokyo, Kyoto, and Osaka: Keep conversations at a low volume on public transport. Many locals use this time for quiet reflection or relaxation.

6. Gift Giving:

Tokyo, Kyoto, and Osaka: When presenting a gift, offer it with both hands as a sign of respect. It's common for the recipient to express hesitation before accepting the gift.

7. Chopstick Etiquette:

Tokyo, Kyoto, and Osaka: Avoid sticking chopsticks upright into a bowl of rice, as this resembles a funeral ritual. Do not point or gesture with chopsticks, and refrain from passing food directly from one set of chopsticks to another.

8. Respect for Elders:

Tokyo, Kyoto, and Osaka: Show deference and respect towards elders. Use appropriate honorifics when addressing them and allow them to take precedence in various situations.

9. Public Behavior:

Tokyo, Kyoto, and Osaka: Maintain a level of decorum in public spaces. Loud conversations, public displays of affection, and disruptive behavior are generally frowned upon.

10. Photography Etiquette:

Tokyo, Kyoto, and Osaka: Ask for permission before taking photos of individuals, especially in more intimate or cultural settings. Respect any signs or guidelines regarding photography in certain areas.

11. Tipping Culture:

Tokyo, Kyoto, and Osaka: Tipping is not a common practice in Japan. Exceptional service is considered a standard part of the job, and tipping may even be refused.

12. Recycling and Waste Disposal:

Tokyo, Kyoto, and Osaka: Sort your waste according to local regulations. Recycling is taken seriously, and separating items correctly is appreciated.

13. Onsen Etiquette:

Tokyo, Kyoto, and Osaka (if visiting an onsen): Thoroughly wash and rinse your body before entering the communal bath. Tattoos are often associated with the yakuza, so be aware of onsen policies regarding tattoos.

14. Punctuality:

Tokyo, Kyoto, and Osaka: Punctuality is highly valued. Arrive on time for appointments, tours, and reservations.

15. Noise Levels in Public Places:

Tokyo, Kyoto, and Osaka: Maintain a moderate noise level, especially in public transportation, restaurants, and cultural sites. Use headphones when listening to music or watching videos.

By embracing these cultural etiquette guidelines, you'll not only show respect for Japanese customs but also enhance your overall experience in Tokyo, Kyoto, and Osaka. Observing and adapting to local norms will contribute to positive interactions with the people and culture of Japan.

Dos and Don'ts

Dos:

1. Bow Greetings:

Do: Use a slight bow as a respectful greeting. It's a common and appreciated gesture in various situations.

2. Respect Cultural Customs:

Do: Embrace local customs, such as removing your shoes when entering homes or traditional establishments.

3. Queue Politely:
Do: Form orderly queues in public spaces, especially when waiting for public transport or entering/exiting buildings.

4. Practice Silence on Public Transport:
Do: Keep conversations at a low volume on public transport. Many locals use this time for quiet reflection.

5. Use Honorifics in Speech:
Do: Incorporate honorifics in your speech when addressing others. It shows respect, especially towards elders.

6. Offer Gifts with Both Hands:
Do: When presenting a gift, offer it with both hands. Express humility and gratitude during the exchange.

7. Sort Waste Properly:
Do: Follow local recycling regulations. Sort your waste correctly to contribute to Japan's commitment to environmental sustainability.

8. Ask Permission for Photos:
Do: Ask for permission before taking photos of individuals, particularly in more intimate or cultural settings.

9. Respect Privacy in Onsen:
Do: If visiting an onsen, respect the privacy of others. Thoroughly wash before entering the communal bath.

10. Arrive Punctually:

Do: Value punctuality. Arrive on time for appointments, tours, and reservations.

Don'ts:

1. Avoid Pointing with Chopsticks:

Don't: Point or gesture with chopsticks. Avoid sticking them upright into a bowl of rice, as it resembles a funeral ritual.

2. Don't Tip:

Don't: Tipping is not a common practice in Japan. Exceptional service is considered part of the job.

3. Don't Engage in Loud Behavior:

Don't: Engage in loud conversations, public displays of affection, or disruptive behavior in public spaces.

4. Don't Interrupt Public Silence:

Don't: Break the silence on public transport. Keep conversations hushed and use headphones for personal entertainment.

5. Avoid Disruptive Public Behavior:

Don't: Engage in disruptive behavior in public spaces, cultural sites, or transportation.

6. Don't Disregard Onsen Etiquette:
   Don't: If visiting an onsen, disregard proper etiquette. Thoroughly wash before entering the communal bath and be mindful of onsen policies regarding tattoos.

7. Don't Disrespect Elders:
   Don't: Disrespect elders. Use appropriate honorifics and show deference in various situations.

8. Avoid Tipping Culture:
   Don't: Tipping is not customary. Avoid tipping in restaurants, hotels, or other service establishments.

9. Don't Disregard Local Traditions:
   Don't: Disregard local traditions. Follow customs such as removing shoes when required.

10. Avoid Speaking Loudly in Public:
    Don't: Speak loudly in public spaces. Maintain a moderate noise level to respect others.

Adhering to these dos and don'ts will help you navigate the cultural nuances of Tokyo, Kyoto, and Osaka, ensuring a respectful and positive experience during your travels in Japan.

Greetings and Gestures

1. Greetings:

Common Japanese Greetings:

"Konnichiwa" (こんにちは): A general greeting used throughout the day, meaning "hello" or "good afternoon."

"Ohayou gozaimasu" (おはようございます): Good morning.

"Konbanwa" (こんばんは): Good evening.

"Arigatou gozaimasu" (ありがとうございます): Thank you.

2. Bowing:

Common Gesture: Bowing is a customary form of greeting and showing respect. The depth and duration of the bow may vary based on the formality of the situation. A slight bow is suitable for casual greetings, while a deeper bow is used in more formal settings.

3. Handshakes:

Common Gesture: Handshakes are becoming more common, especially in business settings. However, it's advisable to follow the lead of the Japanese person you are greeting. Some may prefer a bow over a handshake.

4. Exchanging Business Cards:

Common Gesture: When exchanging business cards (meishi), offer and receive them with both hands. Take a moment to study the card before carefully placing it in a cardholder or pocket.

5. Nodding:

Common Gesture: Nodding is a non-verbal way to express agreement or understanding. It is a polite and subtle gesture commonly used in conversations.

6. Verbal Acknowledgment:

Common Gesture: Verbal affirmations such as "Hai" (yes) or "Iie" (no) are used to acknowledge understanding or agreement.

7. Avoid Excessive Physical Contact:

Cultural Norm: Japanese culture tends to avoid excessive physical contact, especially in public. Reserve hugs and kisses for close relationships, and be mindful of personal space.

8. Pointing:

Gesture to Avoid: Pointing at people or objects with your fingers is considered impolite. Instead, use your whole hand to indicate direction or objects.

9. Waving:

Common Gesture: Waving is a friendly gesture, especially in casual situations or to attract someone's attention.

10. Use Polite Language:

Verbal Expression: Use polite language (keigo) when communicating, especially with those you've just met or in formal settings. It demonstrates respect.

11. Eye Contact:

Cultural Norm: Maintain modest eye contact. Prolonged and intense eye contact can be perceived as intrusive or confrontational.

12. Smiling:

Common Gesture: Smiling is generally well-received and appreciated. It conveys warmth and friendliness.

13. Crossing Legs:

Cultural Norm: When sitting, it's customary to cross legs at the ankles rather than at the knees, especially in formal settings.

14. Clapping:

Common Gesture: Clapping is used to show appreciation, especially during performances or ceremonies.

15. Whispering:

Gesture to Avoid: Whispering in public, especially in confined spaces, is generally discouraged. Maintain a moderate volume in conversations.

Embracing these greetings and gestures will enhance your interactions in Tokyo, Kyoto, and Osaka. Remember to be observant of the context and adapt your behavior accordingly to show respect for local customs.

Understanding Japanese Customs

1. Respect for Elders:
   Customary Practice: Show deference and respect towards elders. Use appropriate honorifics when addressing them and allow them to take precedence in various situations.

2. Bowing:
   Customary Practice: Bowing is a common gesture used for greetings, expressing gratitude, or showing respect. The depth and duration of the bow vary based on the formality of the situation.

3. Removing Shoes:
   Cultural Norm: When entering someone's home, traditional ryokans, or certain traditional establishments, it's customary to remove your shoes. Indoor slippers may be provided.

4. Ochugen and Oseibo:
   Customary Practice: Ochugen and Oseibo are gift-giving traditions during specific seasons. Ochugen is typically during midsummer, and Oseibo is around year-end. It's common to give gifts as a token of appreciation.

5. Cherry Blossom Viewing (Hanami):

Cultural Tradition: Hanami is the practice of enjoying cherry blossoms during spring. People gather in parks for picnics under blooming cherry trees, appreciating the transient beauty of the flowers.

6. Tea Ceremony:
Cultural Tradition: The Japanese tea ceremony (茶道, sadō or chanoyu) is a ritualistic preparation, serving, and drinking of matcha (green tea). It emphasizes aesthetics, etiquette, and mindfulness.

7. Seasonal Festivals (Matsuri):
Cultural Tradition: Japan hosts numerous festivals throughout the year, known as matsuri. These events celebrate traditions, history, and local customs. Participating can provide insight into Japanese culture.

8. Gift Wrapping:
Artistic Tradition: Gift wrapping is considered an art form in Japan. The presentation of a gift is crucial, and beautifully wrapped gifts are a sign of thoughtfulness and care.

9. Silence and Harmony:
Cultural Value: Silence is often appreciated, especially in public transport. Japanese culture values harmony, and maintaining a peaceful atmosphere in shared spaces is essential.

10. Respect for Nature:

Cultural Belief: Nature holds a significant place in Japanese culture. Respect for the changing seasons, appreciation for gardens, and the incorporation of natural elements in architecture are common.

11. Group Harmony (Wa):
Cultural Value: Group harmony, known as "wa," is crucial in Japanese society. Consideration for the feelings and opinions of others helps maintain balance and cohesion.

12. Rituals at Shrines and Temples:
Cultural Practice: When visiting shrines or temples, follow rituals such as purification by washing hands and mouth at the chozuya (water ablution pavilion). Respect prayer practices and be mindful of quiet contemplation.

13. Noren Curtains:
Symbolic Decor: Noren curtains are often seen at the entrances of businesses or traditional establishments. They symbolize the transition between public and private spaces.

14. Respect for Personal Space:
Cultural Norm: Japanese people value personal space. Avoid unnecessary physical contact and maintain a comfortable distance when interacting with others.

15. Annual Events and Celebrations:
Cultural Traditions: Participate in annual events like New Year's celebrations, Gion Matsuri in Kyoto, and other local festivals to experience the richness of Japanese traditions.

Understanding and respecting these customs will contribute to a more immersive and positive experience in Tokyo, Kyoto, and Osaka. It shows appreciation for the cultural nuances that make Japan unique.

Useful Japanese Phrases

Embarking on your journey to Tokyo, Kyoto, and Osaka becomes more enriching when you embrace a few essential Japanese phrases. While English is understood in tourist areas, making an effort to communicate in Japanese is highly appreciated by locals. Here are some useful phrases to enhance your travel experience:

Greetings:
1. Konnichiwa (こんにちは): Hello/Good afternoon.
2. Ohayou gozaimasu (おはようございます): Good morning.
3. Konbanwa (こんばんは): Good evening.
4. Oyasumi nasai (おやすみなさい): Good night (before sleep).

Polite Expressions:

5. Arigatou gozaimasu (ありがとうございます): Thank you.

6. Sumimasen (すみません): Excuse me/I'm sorry.

7. Onegaishimasu (お願いします): Please/If you please.

8. Gomen nasai (ごめんなさい): I'm sorry.

Basic Communication:

9. Hai (はい): Yes.

10. Iie (いいえ): No.

11. Watashi wa ____ desu (私は ____ です): I am ____ (fill in with your name or nationality).

12. Eigo o hanasemasu ka? (英語を話せますか?): Do you speak English?

Numbers and Counting:

13. Ichi, ni, san (一, 二, 三): One, two, three.

14. Yon/shi, go, roku (四, 五, 六): Four, five, six.

15. Ju (十): Ten.

16. Hundred (百), Thousand (千): For larger numbers.

Directions:

17. Doko desu ka? (どこですか?): Where is it?

18. Migi (右), Hidari (左): Right, left.

19. Maiban, michi ni mayoimashita (毎晩、道に迷いました): I got lost last night.

Ordering Food:

20. Menu o kudasai (メニューをください): Can I have the menu, please?

21. Oishii desu (美味しいです): It's delicious.

22. Okaikei onegaishimasu (お会計お願いします): Check, please.

Transportation:

23. Eki wa doko desu ka? (駅はどこですか?): Where is the station?

24. Noriba wa doko desu ka? (乗り場はどこですか?): Where is the bus stop?

25. Ikura desu ka? (いくらですか?): How much is it?

Emergency Situations:

26. Tasukete (助けて): Help!

27. Kyuukyuu desu (救急です): Emergency.

28. Denwa o kudasai (電話をください): Please call.

Shopping:

29. Kore wa ikura desu ka? (これはいくらですか?): How much is this?

30. Kaite kudasai (書いてください): Please write it down.

Miscellaneous Phrases:

31. Toire wa doko desu ka? (トイレはどこですか?): Where is the bathroom?

32. Omamori kudasai (お守りください): Can I have a charm/amulet?

33. Tabun, eigo o hanasemasu (たぶん、英語を話せます): Probably, I can speak English.

Chapter 11: Useful Resources:

1. Travel Guides:

Lonely Planet Japan: Comprehensive guides offering insights into various aspects of Japanese culture, travel tips, and city-specific details.

Rough Guides Tokyo, Kyoto & Osaka: Detailed guides providing in-depth information on each city's attractions, accommodations, and local experiences.

2. Language Apps:

Duolingo: Learn basic Japanese phrases and vocabulary through interactive lessons.

Google Translate: Useful for translating text, speech, or images in real-time. Download Japanese language packs for offline use.

3. Transportation Apps:

Hyperdia: Plan train journeys, check schedules, and find the best routes using Japan's extensive rail network.

Google Maps: Navigate public transportation, walking routes, and explore cities with real-time updates.

4. Accommodation Platforms:

Booking.com, Airbnb, and Hotels.com: Explore a variety of accommodation options, from traditional ryokans to modern hotels, and read reviews from other travelers.

5. Weather Apps:

Weather.com or AccuWeather: Stay updated on the latest weather forecasts for Tokyo, Kyoto, and Osaka to plan your activities accordingly.

6. Currency Conversion:

XE Currency Converter: Get real-time currency exchange rates and convert your currency to Japanese yen for a seamless shopping and dining experience.

7. Cultural Insights:

Japan National Tourism Organization (JNTO): Visit their website for cultural insights, travel tips, and updates on events happening during your stay.

8. Local Event Calendars:

Time Out Tokyo, Kyoto, and Osaka: Check event calendars for festivals, exhibitions, and other local events happening during your visit.

9. Local Transportation Cards:

Suica (Tokyo), ICOCA (Kyoto/Osaka): These prepaid smart cards offer convenient access to public transportation, vending machines, and even some stores.

10. Emergency Contacts:

Japan Emergency Services: Familiarize yourself with local emergency contact numbers, including police (110) and ambulance (119).

11. Wi-Fi Connectivity:

Japan Connected-Free Wi-Fi: Find information about Wi-Fi hotspots and connectivity options across the cities.

12. Travel Insurance:

World Nomads or Allianz: Ensure you have comprehensive travel insurance covering medical emergencies, trip cancellations, and other unexpected events.

13. Maps and Guidebooks:

City Maps for Tokyo, Kyoto, and Osaka: Pick up local maps or guidebooks at information centers or use digital maps for easy navigation.

14. Local Apps:

Japan Official Travel App: Developed by JNTO, this app provides travel information, guides, and recommendations for various attractions.

15. Photography Apps:

Instagram and Google Photos: Share your travel experiences and backup photos securely.

Before your trip, download relevant apps and maps for offline use, especially if you anticipate limited internet connectivity. These resources will enhance your travel experience and help you navigate the vibrant cities of Tokyo, Kyoto, and Osaka with confidence.

Maps and Navigation Apps

1. Google Maps:
   Features:
      Real-time navigation for walking, cycling, and public transport.
         Offline maps for areas with limited internet connectivity.
      Detailed information on attractions, restaurants, and businesses.

2. Hyperdia:
   Features:
      Comprehensive rail and transportation schedules for Japan.
      Plan optimal train routes between stations.
      Includes fare information and platform details.

3. Japan Official Travel App:
   Features:
      Maps and guides provided by the Japan National Tourism Organization (JNTO).

Points of interest, attractions, and travel information.
Offline maps for various regions in Japan.

4. Tokyo Subway Navigation:
   Features:
   Detailed Tokyo subway maps with station information.
   Provides the shortest and most efficient routes.
   Supports both English and Japanese.

5. Navitime for Japan Travel:
   Features:
   Comprehensive navigation app for public transport, walking, and driving.
   Real-time updates on transportation schedules.
   Offline maps available for various regions.

6. Osaka Amazing Pass App:
   Features:
   Designed specifically for travelers in Osaka.
   Maps, attraction details, and transportation information.
   Works offline for essential information.

7. Kyoto Official Travel Guide:
   Features:
   Maps and guides curated for Kyoto visitors.
   Information on historical sites, attractions, and cultural experiences.
   Offline functionality for specific content.

8. Japan Travel by NAVITIME:

Features:

Covers multiple cities including Tokyo, Kyoto, and Osaka.

Route planning for public transport, walking, and driving.

Offline maps available for various regions.

9. Tokyo Handy Guide:

Features:

Maps and guides tailored for Tokyo travelers.

Offline access to essential information.

Points of interest, dining, and shopping recommendations.

10. Japan Transit Planner by Jorudan:

Features:

Transit planning for trains, buses, and walking routes.

Real-time updates on schedules and delays.

Covers major cities and regions.

11. Rakuten Travel:

Features:

Focuses on accommodation and hotel booking.

Maps, reviews, and booking options for various budgets.

Useful for planning and navigating to your lodging.

12. Weather Apps with Maps:
    Weather.com or AccuWeather: Check the weather conditions and forecasts with interactive maps for Tokyo, Kyoto, and Osaka.

Before your trip, download these apps and offline maps to ensure smooth navigation, especially in areas with limited internet connectivity. Whether you're exploring the bustling streets of Tokyo, the historical sites of Kyoto, or the vibrant cityscape of Osaka, these navigation apps will enhance your travel experience in Japan.

Language Translation Tools

Navigating Tokyo, Kyoto, and Osaka becomes more seamless when armed with language translation tools, especially if you're not fluent in Japanese. While English is widely used in tourist areas, having translation assistance can enhance your interactions and make your trip more enjoyable. Here are some essential language translation tools:

1. Google Translate:
  Features:
    Real-time translation for text, speech, and images.
    Download language packs for offline use.
        Conversation mode for instant bilingual communication.

2. Microsoft Translator:
Features:
    Speech-to-speech translation with multiple language support.
    Phrasebooks for common travel expressions.
    Offline translation for certain languages.

3. Papago (by Naver):
Features:
        Translation tool developed by South Korean company Naver.
    Supports various languages including Japanese.
    Speech translation and offline mode available.

4. iTranslate:
Features:
    Voice and text translation in multiple languages.
    Offline mode for basic translations without internet access.
    Pronunciation guides for learning key phrases.

5. SayHi Translate:
Features:
        Speech-to-speech translation with a conversational feel.
    Support for multiple languages, including Japanese.
    Can translate written text and spoken words.

6. TripLingo:

Features:

Customized phrasebooks for specific travel situations.

Voice translation and offline access available.

Culture and etiquette tips for various destinations.

7. Babylon Translator:

Features:

Translation tool with support for multiple languages.

Provides definitions, synonyms, and grammar information.

Offline mode for basic translation needs.

8. Yandex.Translate:

Features:

Translation tool developed by Russian company Yandex.

Supports various languages, including Japanese.

Offline mode for basic translations.

9. Waygo:

Features:

Visual translation tool for menus, signs, and printed text.

Focuses on instant translation using your device's camera.

Useful for quick on-the-go translation needs.

10. Translate Voice (by iSpeech):
   Features:
   Speech-to-speech translation with a simple interface.
   Supports multiple languages, including Japanese.
   Offline mode for basic translations without internet access.

11. Easy Language Translator:
   Features:
   Quick and easy text translation tool.
   Supports a wide range of languages.
   Pronunciation guides for learning key phrases.

12. Jisho.org (Online Dictionary):
   Features:
   Online Japanese-English dictionary for quick word lookup.
   Kanji search with stroke order diagrams.
   Useful for understanding signs and written text.

13. Pocketalk:
   Features:
   Dedicated translation device for real-time conversations.
   Multiple language support, including Japanese.
   Connects to Wi-Fi or uses a built-in SIM card for internet access.

14. Speak & Translate:
  Features:
        Speech-to-speech translation with a user-friendly interface.
    Supports multiple languages, including Japanese.
    Offline mode for basic translations.

Before your trip, download your chosen language translation apps and ensure you have the necessary language packs for offline use, especially in areas with limited internet connectivity. These tools will serve as valuable companions, breaking down language barriers and facilitating smooth communication during your exploration of Tokyo, Kyoto, and Osaka.

Travel Apps and Websites

Planning a trip to Tokyo, Kyoto, and Osaka involves a combination of research, navigation, and organization. These travel apps and websites cater to various aspects of your journey, from finding accommodation to exploring local attractions.

1. Booking Platforms:
        Booking.com: Explore a wide range of accommodations, from hotels to guesthouses. Read reviews, check availability, and book directly through the app.

Airbnb: Discover unique stays, including apartments and traditional Japanese homes (ryokans). Connect with local hosts for personalized experiences.

2. Transportation Apps:

Hyperdia: Plan your train journeys with detailed schedules, routes, and fare information. Essential for navigating Japan's extensive rail network.

Google Maps: Navigate public transportation, walking routes, and explore cities with real-time updates. Download offline maps for areas with limited internet connectivity.

3. Currency Conversion:

XE Currency Converter: Get real-time currency exchange rates and convert your currency to Japanese yen for a seamless shopping and dining experience.

4. Local Event Calendars:

Time Out Tokyo, Kyoto, and Osaka: Stay informed about events, festivals, exhibitions, and local happenings. Check event calendars for exciting experiences during your visit.

5. Language Learning Apps:

Duolingo: Learn basic Japanese phrases and vocabulary through interactive lessons before your trip.

Rosetta Stone: Enhance your language skills with immersive lessons and pronunciation practice.

6. Local Apps:

Japan Official Travel App: Developed by the Japan National Tourism Organization (JNTO), this app provides cultural insights, travel tips, and guides for various attractions.

Tokyo Handy Guide: City-specific app offering maps, guides, and essential information for Tokyo visitors.

Kyoto Official Travel Guide: Similar to the Tokyo Handy Guide, but tailored for Kyoto travelers.

Osaka Amazing Pass App: Designed specifically for Osaka visitors, offering maps, guides, and transportation information.

7. Weather Apps:

Weather.com or AccuWeather: Stay updated on the latest weather forecasts for Tokyo, Kyoto, and Osaka to plan your activities accordingly.

8. Photography Apps:

Instagram and Google Photos: Share your travel experiences, discover local spots, and backup photos securely.

9. Japan Transit Planner by Jorudan:

Features:

Transit planning for trains, buses, and walking routes.

Real-time updates on schedules and delays.

Covers major cities and regions.

10. Rakuten Travel:
Features:
Focuses on accommodation and hotel booking.
Maps, reviews, and booking options for various budgets.
Useful for planning and navigating to your lodging.

11. World Nomads or Allianz (Travel Insurance):
Ensure you have comprehensive travel insurance covering medical emergencies, trip cancellations, and other unexpected events.

12. Wi-Fi Connectivity:
Japan Connected-Free Wi-Fi: Find information about Wi-Fi hotspots and connectivity options across the cities.

13. Google Translate:
Essential for translating text, speech, or images in real-time. Download Japanese language packs for offline use.

14. Maps and Guidebooks:
City Maps for Tokyo, Kyoto, and Osaka: Pick up local maps or guidebooks at information centers or use digital maps for easy navigation.

15. Health and Wellness Apps:
MyFitnessPal or Headspace: Maintain your well-being with fitness tracking or meditation apps during your travels.

Chapter 12: Photography Tips and Perfect Spots

Capturing the essence of Tokyo, Kyoto, and Osaka through photography is an exciting way to preserve your travel memories. Here are some photography tips and suggested spots to help you create stunning images:

Photography Tips:

1. Golden Hours: Capture the cities during the golden hours (sunrise and sunset) for warm and soft lighting. It adds a magical touch to your photos.

2. City Lights: Explore the vibrant cityscapes at night. Tokyo, in particular, comes alive with neon lights. Long exposure shots can create dynamic and colorful scenes.

3. Seasonal Shots: Leverage the beauty of each season. Cherry blossoms in spring, colorful foliage in autumn, and snow-covered landscapes in winter provide unique photo opportunities.

4. Street Photography: Embrace the bustling streets and capture the energy of daily life. Candid shots of people, local markets, and street performers showcase the city's authenticity.

5. Architectural Wonders: Tokyo's modern skyscrapers, Kyoto's traditional machiya houses, and Osaka's contemporary architecture offer diverse subjects for architectural photography.

6. Traditional Elements: Seek out traditional elements like torii gates, historic temples, and traditional tea houses in Kyoto. These represent Japan's rich cultural heritage.

7. Reflections: Utilize water features for reflections. The iconic reflections in Tokyo's waterways or Kyoto's serene gardens can add a poetic dimension to your photos.

8. Explore Districts: Each city has distinct districts. Capture the contrasting atmospheres of Shibuya's bustling streets, Kyoto's historic Gion, and Osaka's vibrant Dotonbori.

9. Framing: Use natural elements like trees, doorways, or bridges to frame your subjects. It adds depth and focus to your photos.

10. Capture Festivals: If your visit aligns with local festivals, immerse yourself in the celebrations and capture the vibrant colors and cultural performances.

Perfect Photography Spots:

Tokyo:
1. Shibuya Crossing: Iconic pedestrian crossing with a sea of people and illuminated billboards.
2. Tokyo Tower: Capture this iconic landmark against the city skyline.
3. Asakusa Senso-ji Temple: Traditional architecture with the Thunder Gate (Kaminarimon) as a picturesque entrance.
4. Odaiba Seaside Park: Stunning views of Tokyo Bay and the Rainbow Bridge.

Kyoto:
1. Fushimi Inari Taisha: Endless torii gates create a unique pathway, especially during early morning or late afternoon.
2. Kinkaku-ji (Golden Pavilion): The shimmering golden exterior surrounded by reflecting ponds.
3. Arashiyama Bamboo Grove: A surreal bamboo forest providing an enchanting atmosphere.
4. Kiyomizu-dera: Panoramic views of Kyoto from the wooden terrace.

Osaka:
1. Dotonbori Canal: Neon lights, vibrant signs, and reflections in the canal create a lively atmosphere.
2. Osaka Castle: Majestic castle surrounded by cherry blossoms in spring.
3. Kuromon Ichiba Market: Capture the vibrant colors of fresh produce and street food stalls.

4. Umeda Sky Building: Photograph Osaka's skyline from the Floating Garden Observatory.

Remember to respect local customs and regulations while taking photos, especially in sacred or private areas. Experiment with different angles and perspectives to add variety to your photo collection. Whether you're capturing the modernity of Tokyo, the historical charm of Kyoto, or the dynamic energy of Osaka, these photography tips and spots will help you create lasting memories of your Japanese adventure.

Hiring Photographer

If you want to ensure professional and memorable photos of your journey through Tokyo, Kyoto, and Osaka, hiring a local photographer can be a fantastic idea. Here are some steps to help you find and hire the right photographer for your needs:

1. Research:
    Photographer Directories: Explore online photographer directories or platforms like Google My Business, Yelp, or specialized photography websites.
    Social Media: Browse through Instagram, Facebook, or photography forums to discover local photographers showcasing their work.

2. Portfolio Review:

Websites and Portfolios: Visit photographers' websites or online portfolios to review their style, expertise, and previous work.

Specialization: Look for photographers with experience in the type of photography you desire, whether it's portrait, landscape, or event photography.

3. Reviews and Testimonials:

Client Reviews: Check for client reviews and testimonials to gauge the photographer's professionalism, communication, and the quality of the final images.

Social Proof: Look for social media comments and reviews from previous clients.

4. Contact and Communication:

Email or Messaging: Initiate contact through email or messaging to discuss your requirements, dates, and any specific requests.

Response Time: Assess the photographer's responsiveness and communication style.

5. Discuss Expectations:

Style Preferences: Clearly communicate your preferred photography style, whether it's candid, posed, or a mix of both.

Locations and Spots: Discuss specific locations and landmarks you want to include in your photo session.

6. Pricing and Packages:

Quote Request: Request a detailed quote, including pricing, packages, and any additional costs.

Customization: Check if the photographer offers customizable packages to suit your needs.

7. Confirm Availability:

Dates and Times: Confirm the photographer's availability for your desired dates and times.

Booking Confirmation: Once details are finalized, request a booking confirmation to secure their services.

8. Meet or Virtual Consultation:

Face-to-Face or Virtual Meeting: Arrange a meeting, either in person or virtually, to discuss details, address any questions, and establish a rapport.

Contracts and Agreements: Ensure there's a clear understanding by reviewing and signing a contract that outlines the terms and conditions.

9. Prepare for the Session:

Wardrobe Choices: Coordinate wardrobe choices for your photoshoot based on the locations and themes.

Props or Accessories: Discuss any props or accessories you'd like to include in the photos.

10. Enjoy the Session:

Relax and Have Fun: On the day of the shoot, relax, enjoy the experience, and trust the photographer's expertise.

11. Receive and Review Images:

Delivery Timeline: Confirm the expected timeline for receiving the edited images.

Feedback: Provide feedback on the final images and express your satisfaction.

12. Share the Experience:

Social Media Sharing: If you're pleased with the results, consider sharing your experience on social media platforms to support the photographer's work.

Hiring a local photographer can add a professional touch to your travel memories and ensure you have high-quality images capturing the beauty of Tokyo, Kyoto, and Osaka.

Capturing the Essence of the Cities

To truly capture the essence of Tokyo, Kyoto, and Osaka through your lens, it's essential to embrace the unique blend of modernity and tradition, fast-paced urban life, and serene historical landscapes. Here's a guide to help you infuse your photographs with the spirit of each city:

1. Tokyo: The Dynamic Metropolis:
Shibuya Crossing: Capture the iconic moment when thousands of people cross the world's busiest pedestrian crossing.

Tokyo Skyline: Head to observation decks like Tokyo Tower or Tokyo Skytree for breathtaking views of the cityscape, especially during sunset.

Harajuku Street Fashion: Immerse yourself in the vibrant and eclectic street fashion scene of Harajuku, known for its unique styles and creative expression.

Tsukiji Outer Market: Capture the hustle and bustle of the seafood market, with vendors, chefs, and visitors indulging in culinary delights.

2. Kyoto: Tranquil Beauty and Tradition:
Fushimi Inari Taisha: Photograph the mesmerizing path lined with torii gates, especially during early morning or late afternoon to capture the magical light.

Arashiyama Bamboo Grove: Create enchanting images of the towering bamboo stalks, playing with light and shadows.

Gion District: Stroll through the historic Gion district, capturing the traditional machiya houses, geishas, and lantern-lit streets.

Kinkaku-ji (Golden Pavilion): Reflect the elegance of this golden structure in the surrounding pond.

3. Osaka: A Fusion of Modernity and Tradition:
Dotonbori at Night: Capture the vibrant energy of Osaka's entertainment district with its neon signs, street performers, and the famous Glico running man sign.

Osaka Castle: Frame the majestic Osaka Castle against cherry blossoms in spring or fiery foliage in autumn.

Kuromon Ichiba Market: Document the lively atmosphere of this bustling market with its colorful stalls and delicious street food.

Umeda Sky Building: Photograph Osaka's cityscape from the Floating Garden Observatory, especially during the blue hour.

Tips for All Cities:

Seasonal Sensibilities: Adjust your photography focus based on the season – cherry blossoms in spring, lush greens in summer, vibrant foliage in autumn, and snow-covered landscapes in winter.

Candid Moments: Embrace street photography to capture the candid moments of locals and tourists alike, showcasing the daily life and cultural interactions.

Night Photography: Experiment with long exposure shots in urban areas to capture the city lights, reflections, and a sense of movement.

Historical and Modern Contrasts: Showcase the contrast between ancient temples, shrines, and historic districts against the backdrop of modern skyscrapers and bustling streets.

Natural Elements: Utilize natural elements like water, gardens, and parks to add depth and tranquility to your images.

By understanding the unique character of each city and incorporating these tips, you can create a visual narrative that encapsulates the essence of Tokyo's modernity, Kyoto's traditional charm, and Osaka's dynamic fusion of the old and new. Your photographs will not only serve as memories but as a testament to the multifaceted beauty of these captivating Japanese cities.

Responsible Photography

Responsible photography is crucial to ensure that your exploration of Tokyo, Kyoto, and Osaka respects local cultures, traditions, and the privacy of individuals. Here are some guidelines to follow for ethical and respectful photography:

1. Respect Cultural and Religious Sites:
    No Flash Photography: Avoid using flash in places of worship, museums, and historic sites, as it can damage artifacts and disturb the atmosphere.
    Observe Rules and Signs: Follow posted guidelines and signs regarding photography restrictions. Some areas may prohibit photography altogether.

2. Ask for Permission:
    Portraits and Close-ups: Request permission before taking close-up shots of individuals, especially in markets, neighborhoods, or cultural events.
    Respect Personal Space: Be aware of personal space and cultural norms when photographing people in public spaces.

3. Be Mindful of Privacy:

Avoid Intrusion: Refrain from photographing individuals without their consent in private or intimate settings.

Children and Vulnerable Groups: Exercise caution when photographing children and vulnerable groups to protect their privacy and well-being.

4. Preserve Nature and Wildlife:

No Feeding or Disturbing Wildlife: Avoid feeding or disturbing animals for the sake of a photograph. Maintain a safe distance in natural environments.

Stay on Designated Paths: Follow designated paths and respect nature reserves to minimize your impact on the environment.

5. Leave No Trace:

Pack Out What You Pack In: Dispose of your trash responsibly and avoid leaving any waste behind, especially in natural areas.

Respect Local Property: Do not climb on private property or restricted areas for the sake of a photograph.

6. Consider the Local Community:

Noise and Disturbance: Minimize noise disruptions during events, festivals, or in residential areas.

Support Local Businesses: If you capture images of local businesses, consider supporting them and showcasing the positive aspects of the community.

7. Educate Yourself on Local Customs:

Dress Modestly: Respect local dress codes, especially when visiting religious or traditional sites.

Know Local Customs: Be aware of cultural sensitivities and practices, such as when and where it is appropriate to take photographs.

8. Avoid Exploitative Imagery:

Dignity and Respect: Do not capture or share images that exploit vulnerable populations or portray individuals in a demeaning manner.

Consider the Impact: Reflect on how your images may be perceived and the potential consequences for the subjects involved.

9. Respect Privacy Laws:

Understand Local Regulations: Be aware of local privacy laws and regulations regarding photography. Avoid taking photos in areas where it is expressly prohibited.

10. Share Positive Stories:

Celebrate Culture: Use your photography to showcase the positive aspects of the local culture, traditions, and community.

Promote Responsible Tourism: Encourage others to be responsible and respectful photographers by setting a positive example.

Chapter 13: Social and Romantic Activities

Whether you're exploring with friends, a significant other, or on your own, Tokyo, Kyoto, and Osaka offer a diverse range of social and romantic activities. Here are some suggestions for creating memorable experiences in each city:

Tokyo: The Modern Metropolis:

1. Robot Restaurant Show (Shinjuku): Immerse yourself in a futuristic and entertaining dining experience with a robot-themed show.

2. Sumida River Cruise (Asakusa): Enjoy a romantic boat ride along the Sumida River, passing by iconic landmarks like Tokyo Skytree and Asakusa.

3. Tsukiji Fish Market Cooking Class: Join a cooking class to learn how to prepare traditional Japanese dishes using fresh ingredients from the famous Tsukiji Fish Market.

4. Odaiba Seaside Park (Odaiba): Take a leisurely stroll along the waterfront, enjoying the view of Rainbow Bridge and the cityscape.

5. Tokyo DisneySea: Embark on a magical day at DisneySea, known for its romantic atmosphere and unique attractions.

Kyoto: The Cultural Gem:

1. Philosopher's Path: Walk hand in hand along the cherry blossom-lined Philosopher's Path, especially stunning during spring.

2. Tea Ceremony Experience: Share a traditional Japanese tea ceremony, immersing yourselves in the rituals and tranquility.

3. Arashiyama Romantic Train Ride: Board the Sagano Romantic Train for a scenic journey through the picturesque Arashiyama bamboo groves.

4. Higashiyama District: Wander through the historic Higashiyama District, exploring traditional shops, teahouses, and narrow cobblestone streets.

5. Boat Ride in Fushimi: Uji River Cruise: Enjoy a serene boat ride along the Uji River in Fushimi, surrounded by greenery and historic sites.

Osaka: The Culinary Haven:

1. Dotonbori River Cruise: Cruise along the neon-lit Dotonbori Canal at night, taking in the lively atmosphere and iconic signs.

2. Kuromon Ichiba Market Stroll: Explore the bustling market together, sampling local street food and delicacies.

3. Osaka Castle Park Cherry Blossom Viewing: Have a romantic picnic during cherry blossom season in the beautiful Osaka Castle Park.

4. Spa World (Shinsekai): Relax and unwind in the themed baths and saunas of Spa World, offering a unique spa experience.

5. Osaka Aquarium Kaiyukan: Share a mesmerizing visit to Kaiyukan, one of the largest aquariums in the world, showcasing diverse marine life.

General Romantic Activities:

1. Rooftop Bars: Tokyo, Kyoto, and Osaka boast stunning rooftop bars with panoramic city views. Perfect for a romantic evening.

2. Traditional Ryokan Stay: Experience Japanese hospitality with a stay at a traditional ryokan, complete with tatami mats and kaiseki meals.

3. Hot Springs (Onsen): Indulge in a relaxing onsen experience. There are numerous hot spring resorts near each city.

4. Ghibli Museum (Mitaka, Tokyo): Explore the whimsical world of Studio Ghibli together in this enchanting museum.

5. Romantic Gardens: Visit beautiful gardens like Shinjuku Gyoen (Tokyo), Kiyomizu-dera (Kyoto), and Kema Sakuranomiya Park (Osaka).

These activities cater to various preferences, from cultural experiences and scenic strolls to vibrant city life and intimate moments. Tailor your itinerary to your interests and create lasting memories in these captivating Japanese cities.

Charming Love and Romantic spots

For those seeking enchanting and romantic experiences, Tokyo, Kyoto, and Osaka offer a plethora of charming spots. Whether you're celebrating a special occasion or simply creating beautiful memories, here are some delightful places to explore:

Tokyo: Love in the Modern Metropolis:

1. Tokyo Tower Illuminations: Enjoy the romantic ambiance created by Tokyo Tower's evening illuminations. The view from nearby parks adds to the charm.

2. Tokyo Metropolitan Government Building Observatory: Capture breathtaking sunset views of the cityscape and beyond from the free observation decks.

3. Roppongi Hills Mori Garden: Stroll hand in hand through this serene garden, an oasis of greenery amid the urban hustle of Roppongi.

4. Sky Circus Sunshine 60 Observatory: Experience a 360-degree panoramic view of Tokyo from this unique observatory in Ikebukuro.

5. Odaiba Seaside Park's "Love Lock" Area: Seal your love by attaching a padlock to the designated area, overlooking Rainbow Bridge.

Kyoto: Romance Amidst Tradition:

1. Kiyomizu-dera: Visit this iconic temple, known for its wooden terrace with panoramic views. The evening illuminations add a touch of magic.

2. Kifune Shrine: Explore the charming Kifune Shrine, especially enchanting during the evening when lanterns illuminate the pathways.

3. Gion Shirakawa Canal: Take a romantic stroll along the canal, lined with willow trees, traditional tea houses, and the iconic Gion district.

4. Hananomai Ryokan Kyoto: Experience a romantic ryokan stay with a private open-air bath and traditional kaiseki dinner.

5. Bamboo Forest in Arashiyama: Wander through the enchanting bamboo groves hand in hand, creating a whimsical atmosphere.

Osaka: Love and Culinary Delights:

1. Umeda Sky Building Floating Garden Observatory: Enjoy a romantic dinner with stunning views at the top of this iconic skyscraper.

2. Osaka Mint Bureau Cherry Blossom Path: During cherry blossom season, the Mint Bureau opens its gates for a magical, romantic stroll.

3. Kitashinchi District: Explore the upscale Kitashinchi area with its sophisticated bars and restaurants for a delightful evening.

4. Nakanoshima Rose Garden: Experience the beauty of over 3,700 roses in bloom, creating a romantic setting in the heart of Osaka.

5. Osaka City Hall Sakura Light-Up: Witness the cherry blossoms beautifully illuminated at Osaka City Hall during the spring season.

General Romantic Tips:

1. Sunset Cruises: Tokyo Bay, Uji River in Kyoto, and Osaka's Dotonbori Canal offer scenic sunset cruises for a romantic evening.

2. Candlelit Dinners: Book a candlelit dinner at one of the many romantic restaurants in each city.

3. Hidden Gems: Seek out lesser-known spots and hidden gardens for a more intimate atmosphere.

4. Seasonal Festivals: Attend seasonal festivals together for a unique and lively experience.

5. Starry Nights: Head to a planetarium for a celestial date night, offering a romantic escape from the city lights.

Remember to check seasonal events and plan your visits accordingly to enhance the romantic atmosphere. Whether it's a magical evening in Tokyo, a traditional rendezvous in Kyoto, or a culinary adventure in Osaka, these charming spots promise to create lasting memories with your loved one.

Tips for Couple Travellers

Traveling as a couple offers a unique opportunity to create shared memories and strengthen your bond. Here are some tips to make your journey through Tokyo, Kyoto, and Osaka as a couple enjoyable and memorable:

1. Plan Together:
Discuss Priorities: Sit down and discuss both of your interests, priorities, and must-see attractions. Create an itinerary that suits both your preferences.

2. Respect Each Other's Pace:
Flexible Itinerary: Allow for spontaneity and be flexible with your plans. If one of you needs more downtime or wants to explore a specific area, be accommodating.

3. Try Local Cuisine Together:
Food Adventures: Japan is renowned for its diverse culinary scene. Try different local dishes together and explore hidden gems in each city's food landscape.

4. Create Intimate Moments:
Romantic Spots: Seek out romantic spots, rooftop bars, and serene gardens where you can enjoy intimate moments together.

5. Capture Memories:

Photography: Take plenty of photos to capture your experiences. It's a wonderful way to create lasting memories of your journey together.

6. Budget Wisely:

Set a Budget: Discuss and set a budget for your trip. This helps in managing expenses and avoiding potential conflicts over money matters.

7. Balance Activities:

Mix of Activities: Plan a mix of activities, from cultural experiences and sightseeing to relaxing moments and leisurely strolls. Find the right balance that suits both your interests.

8. Respect Privacy and Personal Space:

Alone Time: Understand the need for some alone time. Whether it's reading a book, exploring solo for a while, or just enjoying a quiet moment, respect each other's personal space.

9. Stay Connected:

Communication: Keep communication open and honest. Discuss any concerns or preferences to ensure a smooth and enjoyable trip.

10. Experience Local Culture:

Participate in Traditions: Immerse yourselves in local customs, traditions, and cultural experiences. It adds a unique dimension to your journey.

11. Share Responsibilities:
Travel Logistics: Share responsibilities in planning and navigating. It can be fun and collaborative, allowing both of you to contribute to the trip's success.

12. Weather-Appropriate Attire:
Check the Weather: Be prepared for different weather conditions. Check the forecast and pack accordingly to ensure comfort during your explorations.

13. Celebrate Special Occasions:
Plan Ahead: If your trip coincides with a special occasion, plan a surprise or celebrate with a memorable dinner or experience.

14. Learn Basic Local Phrases:
Language: Learn some basic Japanese phrases to enhance your interactions with locals and navigate more comfortably.

15. Relax and Enjoy:
Quality Time: Ultimately, the goal is to enjoy quality time together. Relax, savor the moments, and create a travel experience that strengthens your connection.

By incorporating these tips, you can navigate Tokyo, Kyoto, and Osaka as a couple, creating a travel adventure filled with shared experiences and romance.

Conclusion

As your journey through Tokyo, Kyoto, and Osaka comes to a close, you find yourselves immersed in a tapestry of experiences that blend tradition, modernity, and the unique charm of each city. This triad of Japanese gems has unfolded before you, revealing a rich tapestry of culture, culinary delights, and captivating landscapes that have deepened the connection between you and your partner.

Tokyo, the dynamic metropolis, has offered a symphony of neon lights, bustling streets, and futuristic wonders. From the iconic Shibuya Crossing to the serene Odaiba Seaside Park, Tokyo has effortlessly balanced its modern allure with moments of tranquility. The city's cultural diversity, vibrant street scenes, and cutting-edge innovations have woven a narrative of excitement and discovery for you both.

Kyoto, the cultural gem, has enchanted you with its timeless beauty and traditional charm. Strolling through the historic Gion district, exploring the bamboo groves of Arashiyama, and witnessing the elegance of Kiyomizu-dera, Kyoto has been a canvas painted with the hues of history and nature. Its serene gardens, historic landmarks, and tea ceremonies have provided a serene backdrop for moments of reflection and connection.

Osaka, the culinary haven, has tantalized your taste buds and introduced you to the heart of Kansai hospitality. From the lively Dotonbori district to the tranquil Osaka Mint Bureau Cherry Blossom Path, the city has showcased a vibrant blend of modern entertainment and natural beauty. Osaka's renowned street food, bustling markets, and cultural attractions have created a sensorial journey for you and your partner.

As a couple, you've navigated the complexities of travel, finding a harmonious balance between shared experiences and individual exploration. The local cuisine has become a culinary adventure, each meal telling a story of regional flavors and culinary artistry. The hidden gems you discovered, the romantic spots you cherished, and the cultural encounters you embraced have woven a tapestry of memories that will forever be etched in your hearts.

In crafting your journey, you've embraced responsible photography, respecting local customs, privacy, and the environment. Your travels have been marked by romantic moments, social explorations, and intimate discoveries that transcend the typical tourist experience.

As you bid farewell to Tokyo's skyscrapers, Kyoto's temples, and Osaka's lively streets, you carry with you not just souvenirs and photographs but a shared narrative that has deepened your connection as a couple. The vibrant energy of Tokyo, the timeless elegance of

Kyoto, and the culinary delights of Osaka have left an indelible imprint on your travel story.

In conclusion, your couple's journey through Tokyo, Kyoto, and Osaka has been a symphony of cultural exploration, romantic escapades, and shared adventures. The blend of tradition and modernity, coupled with your respectful engagement with the local communities, has created a travel experience that transcends the ordinary. As you embark on your onward journey, the memories forged in these captivating cities will serve as a testament to the magic of travel, the beauty of shared exploration, and the enduring power of love.

Reflecting on Your Journey

As you pause to reflect on your transformative journey through Tokyo, Kyoto, and Osaka, the tapestry of experiences woven across these captivating cities unfolds before you. Your footsteps have traced a path through a kaleidoscope of cultures, landscapes, and moments that have left an indelible mark on your travel narrative.

Tokyo, the pulsating heart of modernity, welcomed you with open arms and a skyline adorned with dazzling lights. The dynamic energy of Shibuya Crossing, the futuristic allure of Odaiba Seaside Park, and the panoramic views from Tokyo Tower have painted a vivid portrait of a city that never sleeps. Tokyo's kaleidoscope of districts, each with its unique character, offered a mosaic of urban adventures, from the fashionable streets of Harajuku to the historic charm of Asakusa.

Kyoto, the cultural gem, enchanted you with its timeless elegance and a seamless blend of tradition and tranquility. The iconic Fushimi Inari Taisha with its torii gate pathway, the enchanting Arashiyama Bamboo Grove, and the historic Gion district unfolded like chapters from a classical tale. Kyoto's gardens, temples, and teahouses became sanctuaries for reflection, allowing you to immerse yourselves in the essence of Japanese history and aesthetics.

Osaka, the culinary haven and dynamic cultural hub of Kansai, charmed you with its lively streets and delectable flavors. From the neon-lit spectacle of Dotonbori to the serene beauty of Osaka Castle Park, the city embraced you with its vibrant contrasts. Osaka's gastronomic delights, showcased in Kuromon Ichiba Market and the city's array of diverse dining experiences, became a culinary odyssey that reflected the heart of Kansai's culinary heritage.

Together, you ventured into hidden alleys, discovered romantic spots, and embraced responsible travel practices that harmonized with the local communities. Your journey was not merely a checklist of attractions but a narrative of connection – with each other, with the locals, and with the essence of these cities.

As you reflect on the snapshots captured in photographs and etched in your memories, you realize that your journey was not just about the places you visited but the moments you shared. The laughter echoing through bustling markets, the quiet contemplation in temple gardens, and the taste of unfamiliar delicacies became the threads that intertwined to form the fabric of your unique travel story.

In these cities, you didn't just observe; you immersed yourselves in the rhythm of everyday life, becoming a part of the vibrant tapestry of Tokyo, Kyoto, and Osaka. The locals you encountered, the cultural nuances you embraced, and the culinary delights you savored have become threads in the rich tapestry of your journey.

As you move forward, the echoes of your footsteps through these cities will remain with you – a reminder of the beauty of exploration, the power of shared experiences, and the lasting impact of a journey that transcends the ordinary. Tokyo, Kyoto, and Osaka have not just been destinations; they've been companions in your quest for discovery, cultural understanding, and the art of travel.

Leaving Japan with Memories

As your time in Japan draws to a close, the bittersweet feeling of departure is accompanied by a treasure trove of cherished memories that will forever be etched in your hearts. Tokyo, Kyoto, and Osaka have not just been destinations; they've been the canvas upon which your shared journey unfolded, painting a picture of cultural richness, culinary delights, and moments of profound connection.

Tokyo, the vibrant metropolis that pulses with energy, bids you farewell with the echoes of bustling streets and the mesmerizing glow of neon lights. The memories of crossing Shibuya Crossing amidst a sea of people, taking in panoramic views from Tokyo Tower, and strolling through serene parks in Odaiba will remain vivid in your minds. Tokyo's dynamic spirit has imprinted itself on your journey, leaving you with a sense of awe and appreciation for its modernity and tradition seamlessly coexisting.

Kyoto, the timeless cultural gem, whispers its farewells through the rustling leaves of bamboo groves and the echoes of footsteps along historic paths. The torii gates of Fushimi Inari Taisha, the tranquility of Arashiyama's bamboo forest, and the traditional beauty of Gion's streets have become the chapters of a story that unfolded in a city steeped in history and reverence. Kyoto's grace and elegance have left you with a profound appreciation for the essence of Japanese heritage.

Osaka, the culinary haven and vibrant cultural hub, bids you adieu with the sizzling sounds of street food stalls and the laughter echoing in its lively districts. The taste of delicacies from Kuromon Ichiba Market, the enchantment of cherry blossoms in Osaka Castle Park, and the dynamic atmosphere of Dotonbori have become the flavors and rhythms that define your Osaka experience. The city's culinary diversity and vibrant street life have left an imprint on your palate and a sense of the city's pulsating heartbeat.

As you board your departure flight, the memories you carry are not just snapshots in a photo album but a collection of moments that have woven themselves into the fabric of your shared history. The laughter over bowls of ramen, the quiet contemplation in ancient temples, and the warmth of interactions with locals have become the intangible souvenirs that transcend time and space.

Japan, with its blend of tradition and innovation, has offered you a tapestry of experiences that goes beyond sightseeing. It has been a journey of shared discovery, cultural immersion, and the kindling of a deeper connection. The people you encountered, the flavors you savored, and the landscapes you explored have become the threads that bind your memories together.

As the airplane ascends into the skies, Tokyo's skyscrapers, Kyoto's temples, and Osaka's vibrant streets become distant specks on the horizon. Yet, the essence of Japan travels with you, carried in your hearts and memories. Leaving Japan is not the end of a chapter; it's a continuation of a story that will be recounted with fondness, shared with loved ones, and revisited in the quiet moments of reflection.

Japan, with its cultural tapestry and warm hospitality, has become a part of your journey, and the memories crafted within its borders will forever hold a special place in the chronicles of your travels. As you bid sayonara to the Land of the Rising Sun, you carry with you not just the physical mementos but the intangible essence of a transformative sojourn that has enriched your lives. Until next time, Japan, with gratitude and a heart full of memories, you are left with a profound sense of appreciation for the beauty and depth that travel can bring.

Happy Travels!

Made in the USA
Las Vegas, NV
30 June 2024

91681070R00154